giraffe MONEY ESSENTIALS

7 Simple Paths to Build Wealth ***FASTER***

FREE BONUS

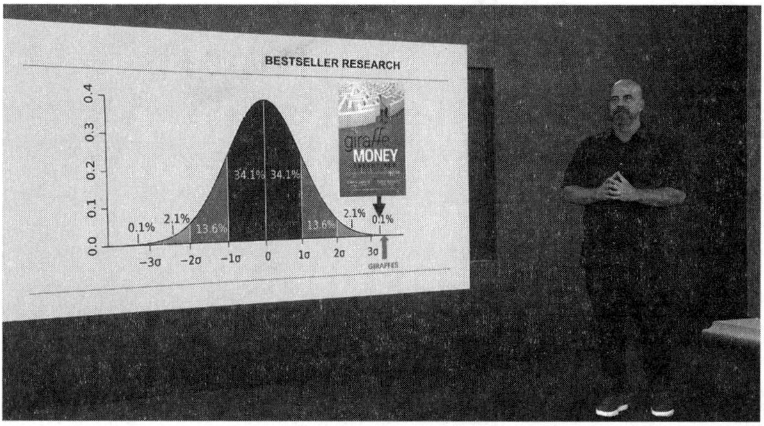

We wrote *giraffeMONEY Essentials* to show you that wealth building, asset protection, and estate planning don't need to be complicated, time-consuming, or expensive.

A small number of financial decisions can have an amazing impact on your long-term financial plan. To help you on your journey, we offer you these free bonus items:

- Video training, explaining how to get the most out of *giraffeMONEY Essentials*
- Exercises and worksheets
- Assessment tools for you, your family, and your business
- E-newsletter subscription
- Useful links
- **No-cost, no-obligation consultation ($500 value)**

You get everything at www.ChrisJarvis.me/money/bonus or by scanning the QR Code below

Bonus Stuff

www.ChrisJarvis.me/money/bonus

"I love Chris' brilliant intellect, wonderful sense of humor, and no-BS approach to business and life. Chris is first and foremost a teacher who wants to help people by eliminating the unnecessary stress and aggravation around money. His motives are pure, and his advice is unbiased and invaluable."

JACK CANFIELD
World's #1 Success Coach,
Founder of the billion-dollar Chicken Soup for the Soul® publishing empire

"I have been in the financial services industry for almost fifty years. Tony's book, ***giraffeMONEY Essentials***, gives a novel and unique approach to creating a long-term financial plan that helps people achieve their wealth accumulation goals. This book is a must-read for people who are serious about reaching higher!"

GARY T. (DOC) HUFFMAN
Retired President and CEO Ohio National Financial Services,
Retired President LIMRA, Retired President of the American College

"In forty years of working with accountants, lawyers, and consultants, I have never met someone with as broad a knowledge base and exceptional creativity as Chris. Having a high-priced team of professional firms working for you doesn't mean you are getting the best possible advice. He has helped me, my company, and my family immensely. I highly recommend you talk to Chris and see what you might be missing."

GORDON LOGAN
Founder and Chairman of SportClips,
International Franchise Association Entrepreneur of the Year,
and Hall of Fame Award Recipient

"***giraffeMONEY Essentials*** stands as a beacon of innovative wisdom. It uniquely combines rigorous financial analysis with imaginative 'giraffe' lessons and a touch of humor. Assadi & Jarvis don't just guide us through the mechanics of wealth-building—they invite us to rethink its purpose and our relationship with it. A must-read for anyone serious about crafting a meaningful financial future."

ROSEANNA DEMARIA
Adjunct Professor, New York University, Founder of DeMaria Group,
Former First Vice President, Merrill Lynch

"Jarvis is the proverbial man with the plan; the sort of financial fixer that one sees in movies and television shows."

HONORABLE ANDREW L. BRASHER
U.S. Circuit Judge, United States Court of Appeals, Eleventh Circuit

"Financial advice and planning is an underrated profession. I've spent my career in the financial services industry, and I can say without any equivocation that Tony Assadi's acumen as a wealth management practitioner is unsurpassed. ***giraffeMONEY Essentials*** offers a blueprint on the undervalued virtues of financial advice and planning. Kudos to Assadi for extolling his wisdom and expertise."

SEAN N. WOODROFFE
EVP, Chief People, Culture & Communications Officer, Lincoln Financial

"I met Chris at a national meeting, and I was immediately interested in what he had to say. After several consultations, and a myriad of questions, we created a financial plan that I have carefully followed. This comprehensive plan includes retirement planning, estate planning and tax management. It has created a clear path for me to financial success—the way I define success. Before meeting Chris, I was working without a clear goal in mind. Now I have targeted milestones and have a great deal of confidence in what my financial future holds. I have found Chris to be honest, forthright, and easy to work with. I'd encourage anyone with financial questions to engage Chris and see if there is a mutual fit."

DR. DAVID KAUFMAN
Founder of The Natural Result, Former Navy SEAL

"***giraffeMONEY Essentials*** simplifies complex financial concepts into easily digestible content, making it a great resource for beginners and experts. The inclusion of interactive, workbook-like elements helps bridge the gap between theory and implementation. It's a great book that all financial enthusiasts should have on their shelves."

DR. COLIN SLABACH, PhD, CFP®
New York University Professor and Founding Faculty for the Master's in Financial Planning Program

“I’ve known, and worked closely with, Chris Jarvis for over twenty years. What most people recognize about Chris are his creative financial and business skills (both of which are truly unique). But his most unique gifts are his genuine concern for others and his willingness and ability to help solve problems. Chris has helped me to look at my firm and my career from different perspectives. He was an invaluable resource helping me prepare my company for an eight-figure exit. I recommend Chris without reservation to any business or business owner looking for an ally who can make a meaningful impact.”

DAN ACETI
35-year financial services executive

“Rapid technological changes will shape the landscape of finance and banking over the next decade. Smaller companies that embrace the idea of leaving the herd and doing things differently, like the giraffe does, can take market share from much larger firms that are slow to adapt. ***giraffeMONEY Essentials*** is a must read for all our managers and leaders so they can better understand and serve our clients’ changing needs.”

SHANA DE PAOLI
Co-CEO and Chairman of the Board, UBank

“Chris has been an invaluable asset to my company, my family and me. He takes the time to understand the real concerns, asks the tough questions most people won’t, and brings very creative solutions. He communicates well with our other advisers, our management team, and our family members. Working with Chris was a great investment on my part.”

CHRIS MAY
CEO, IE Discovery

“The focus for Tony isn’t on himself; he focuses on others and making their lives better. That’s at the core of ***giraffeMONEY Essentials***! The blending of financial planning with emotional intelligence and practicality make this book invaluable. Organized with checklists and summaries, it provides lifelong reference and a pathway to living a better life!”

ED BONACH
Retired Insurance Executive

"An enormously gifted speaker and writer, Chris is the ultimate teacher's teacher. He's exceptionally creative, insightful, articulate, wise, and passionate. His purpose-driven approach simply sees problems differently and, accordingly, solves them with an elegant simplicity. When I'm struggling with how to think through a challenge or communicate a topic, he's the one I call. I'm profoundly grateful to call him my friend."

CHRIS ERBLICH, ESQ.
Partner, Husch Blackwell, LLP,
Chairman and CEO, TFO Family Office Partners

"I have been in insurance for over twenty-five years, working with some of the brightest minds. Chris is one of the smartest and most creative people I know. He has a unique ability to simplify complicated concepts and provide guidance. More importantly, Chris is a terrific person who is always thinking of others. Whenever I face a challenge, he is one of the people I call first. I am honored to call him a friend and colleague."

DAN STANLEY
VP Life Operations, Lion Street

"The best presentation I have heard in forty-three years! His expertise as a business consultant and financial advisor gives him a unique perspective that make his training meetings valuable, memorable, and forward-focused."

TOM ARCHER
CEO, Elite Marketing Group. Former Chairman,
Insurance Designers of America

"As a TEDx organizer, I have worked with hundreds of successful speakers. Unsurprisingly, 'Mr. Giraffe' Chris Jarvis stands out among them all—and not because his talk went viral. The value of his advice and his genuine concern have helped me professionally and personally. He's the real deal: walking the walk and talking the talk. I'm honored to call him a friend."

GARY DOHERTY
Derry Londonderry TEDx Organizer,
International PR Expert

To my enthusiastic co-author Tony,

Thank you for inspiring me to replace a dozen books with the more relatable and impactful ***Essentials***.

Your excitement made this book what it is.

—CHRIS

To my parents, Janet and Mehran, who taught me that the most important currency is making meaning in life through doing good, being good, and making good.

—TONY

Giraffe University Press

ISBN: 978-1-952421-40-2

Printed in the United States of America

CONTENTS

FOREWORD

BY JUSTIN ARMSTRONG

Co-CEO of UBANK

You may be thinking, *Oh great, a bank CEO writing the foreword to a financial book. This should help me catch up on my sleep.* But this short introduction will be the first of many surprises you will find in ***giraffeMONEY Essentials.***

Think about all the ways your life has changed over the past thirty years. You not only carry a computer, phone, and encyclopedia in your pocket, but we've had fifteen iterations of the iPhone. You can sit on the couch or lie in bed—and use your phone to have groceries delivered to your house in a matter of hours. If you wanted, you could also shop for and buy the car that delivers those groceries. Despite all the conveniences that technology has brought to us, the effect on banking has been the opposite.

If you don't believe me, think about the last few challenges you have had with your bank, credit card, or loan. Has it become easier or harder to get problems resolved? Do you feel ignored or loved after getting lost in the phone tree? When was the last time you had a pleasant interaction with someone from the bank who lives in your town? Do you remember when you used to come home from the bank with a lollipop from the bank teller?

Five years ago, Shana De Paoli and I partnered up to change the face of banking. I joined Shana to pursue the (extremely) audacious goal of transforming UBank from a sleepy East Texas community bank to an innovative financial organization. As a small bank in a small town with fewer resources than the big national and multinational institutions, we quickly concluded that we were going to have to play Moneyball. Since we couldn't compete for the same clients with the same offerings, we had to be willing to stick our necks out—like the giraffe—and try something different.

UBank had to be willing to try things that our competitors wouldn't, embrace technologies our competitors couldn't, and evolve to meet people where they needed us most. In our rapidly changing society, the financial needs of individuals and businesses have changed dramatically, and for the most part, financial institutions have failed to adapt to those needs. If we were to have any chance of success, we would need to reach out to small businesses and figure out what they need most—and perhaps more importantly, *how* they need it!

Being a leader of a community bank in conservative East Texas means that I have the opportunity, and the responsibility, to develop relationships with the bank's employees, customers, and strategic partners. This hands-on leadership experience has taught me many important lessons and brought me in contact with several amazing people. Over the last few years, I have developed a professional admiration and a personal friendship with one of them in particular: Tony Assadi.

In addition to coauthoring ***giraffeMONEY Essentials,*** Tony has made many valuable strategic introductions for the bank and has brought a tailored wealth management experience to the bank's highest profile clients, who range from professional athletes and entertainers to extraordinarily wealthy families that painstakingly strive to remain under the radar. His innovative and refreshing approach to building and sustaining legacies, as opposed to simply managing money, provides unique opportunities for our bank and clients to create real and lasting effects in the communities we touch.

It is an honor to call Tony a friend, but my privilege extends even further considering the purpose and value offered in ***giraffeMONEY Essentials.*** This book aligns with our passion for helping people by meeting them where they want you. In our world of super-sub-specialization, there are forty different kinds of attorneys, nearly a dozen types of accountants, and myriad financial, insurance, and investment advisors. People don't have time to meet with a handful of different advisors, let alone to interview scores of them to find one who understands their needs. ***giraffeMONEY Essentials*** provides a multidisciplinary foundation of information on legal, tax, investment, insurance, and business topics. Further, it lays out practical steps to help individuals, families, and businesses save time and money, remove uncertainty, and mitigate risk.

To us, UBank represents more than a conventional bank, and ***giraffeMONEY Essentials*** isn't conventional wisdom. It surpasses the definition of products, services, physical branches, and digital platforms. It is a community, a collective force larger than any individual within it. We share this not as a cliché or to be trite, but as our genuine mission. The community rallying behind our brand is living and breathing, pioneering into uncharted territories. The fruit of our collective efforts is proof that the whole is indeed greater than the sum of its parts—a sentiment I believe should echo in the essence of every company.

In many industries, the art of consumer consideration and winning by delivering value is often overlooked. Sometimes it simply means saying "no" when necessary or imparting wisdom about financial cornerstones. It involves being transparent about what the customer truly needs. At UBank, we understand the value of having an honest, cohesive team, whether it's a wealth manager, insurance representative, bank, attorney, or accountant. ***giraffeMONEY Essentials*** isn't just an investment book, an insurance book, a legal book, or a tax book; it's all these things, and so much more. It is the essential guide to financial wellness for people from all walks of life.

People bank with people, not just a bank, and likewise, people do business with people, not just a business. After listening to Chris Jarvis's TED Talk ("Surviving Ain't Thriving"), I can confidently say that people shouldn't be working with their financial advisors to survive; they should be working with them to thrive.

Together, let's embark on a journey where financial empowerment transcends generations. ***giraffeMONEY Essentials*** and UBank—united in a mission to turn purpose into lasting impact.

JUSTIN ARMSTRONG

Co-CEO of UBANK

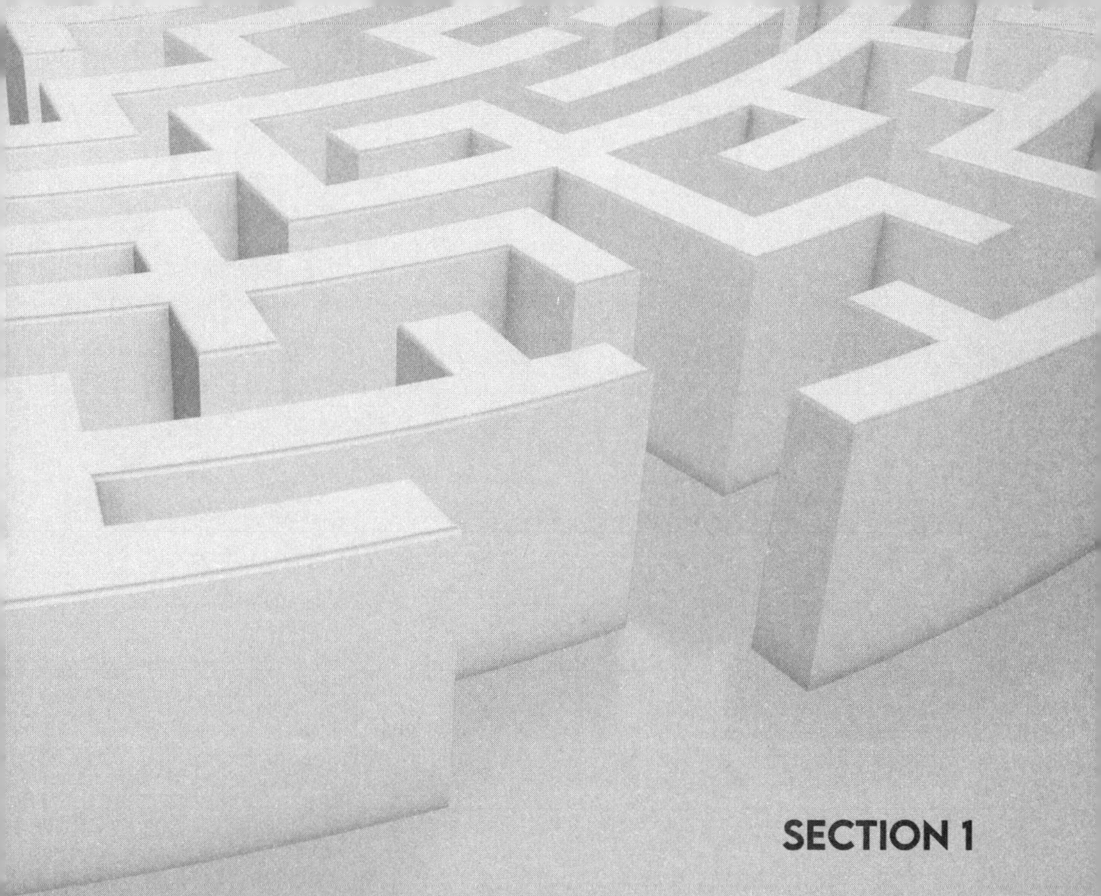

SECTION 1

ELEVATING YOUR PERSPECTIVE

CHAPTER 1

THE MOST IMPORTANT LESSON

TIME IS FREE, BUT IT'S PRICELESS.
YOU CAN'T OWN IT, BUT YOU CAN USE IT.
YOU CAN'T KEEP IT, BUT YOU CAN SPEND IT.
ONCE YOU'VE LOST IT YOU CAN NEVER GET IT BACK.

—HARVEY MACKAY

Over twenty-five years ago, Chris wrote the first of his eighteen books. The early ones were nearly four hundred pages long—and they were dense. The same way jungles host the widest collection of plants and animal species on the planet, these early books included an extensive variety of legal and financial topics. In fairness, the earliest books were written pre-internet when we couldn't access the infinite history of information in the palm of our hands.

Maybe you've heard tales of a prehistoric time when people carried library cards in their wallets, purses, or original fanny packs. In the early 1990s, information was valuable currency in the financial world. Industry insiders were the gatekeepers of knowledge. Without a highly (over) paid broker, you had no way to get an updated stock quote or access any research, let alone make a trade.

Times have changed—so much so that the fanny pack has come full circle and rebranded itself as a waist pouch or belt bag. One day, our kids are ridiculing us for wearing fanny packs. Today, they are "liking" Gucci's utterly ridiculous $2,600 belt bag. Fashion may go in cycles, but technology will only advance. Siri, Google, Alexa, and ChatGPT can deliver thousands of pages of content in a matter of seconds. Once upon a not-that-long-ago, we looked anywhere and everywhere for more information. Today we look away from it. Think about how many emails you delete or ignore without even opening them.

When we began planning the future of ***giraffeMONEY Essentials,*** we realized that we had to first look back. Over the past twenty to thirty years, we have interacted with thousands of clients and thousands of financial, legal, tax, and investment advisors. With the benefit of hindsight, experience and even a little maturity, we noticed something that had previously escaped us.

Ironically, the financial firms and professionals are dealing in borderline worthless currency—and severely overcharging for it. Investment advisors, financial planners, attorneys, and accountants are proudly wielding "information." They (um, we) have been so proud of what we know about this, that, and the other boring thing that we presumed everyone wanted our Confederate dollars. We were wrong.

Clients don't sit down with us to listen to what we have to say. People come to advisors so we can listen to them. They want us to understand them so we can recommend a plan and then implement it—as quickly, as cost-effectively, and as painlessly as possible.

Professionals have it backward—focusing on maximizing billable hours (for ***their*** time) to give you information. Speaking of which, have you noticed the bold—dare we say ballsy—billing rates out there? We just had a first-year lawyer attend one of our live events. He admitted that he doesn't know much, yet the firm bills him out at $650 per hour! Advisors need to evolve to meet the changing needs of clients.

TIME IS MORE VALUABLE THAN MONEY

Information has been replaced by time—your time—as the most valuable commodity. In our one-on-one consulting and mentoring, this belief is universal. When you consider that these clients are often worth $50 million to $100 million, and their time is very valuable, this is one powerful statement!

We are strong believers in a modified Pareto principle. The Pareto principle states that 80% of the work gets done by 20% of the people. Most companies agree that 80% of the profits come from 20% of the products or 20% of the customers. Essentially, not every client, employee, product, or market is created equally. Strategy consulting has become a $100 billion industry based on the application of this principle—and helping firms identify their 20% and formulate plans to spend more time in that more profitable space.

In life, we believe that 10% of the decisions you make account for 90% of the impact. Our coaching and mentoring focus on helping families and businesses spend more time and energy on important decisions and considerably less on the rest. In our firm, Beyond Wealth, our offer is to get 90% of your financial planning done in ninety days. We understand that your time is important; your health is important; your business is important. Finances are merely a vehicle to help you live your life.

We've brought a similar approach to this book. Unlike the jungle books of decades past, we skipped many financial and legal topics—and significantly shortened the explanations of the ones we did include. If you wanted to practice law or become a CFP®, we assume you would have already done it. We appreciate that you don't want to waste your time becoming an expert at something you should only have to do once. Our goal is to maximize your return on life by giving you enough information about twenty or so very impactful tools and strategies that will help you get 90% of your planning done in ninety days.

After all, if you are speaking to your advisors more than your parents or children, something is wrong. Money should not be the reason for your life, but the facilitator of your best life. We hope ***giraffeMONEY Essentials*** will give you the necessary information and practical recommendations so you can put financial planning behind you and get back to doing the things that matter most. Growing your business, spending time with loved ones, and getting a good night's sleep should replace money-related tasks on the to-do list.

CHAPTER 2
YOU'RE NOT ALONE, BUT MAYBE YOU WANT TO BE

I REFUSE TO JOIN ANY CLUB THAT WOULD HAVE ME.

—GROUCHO MARX

As we looked back at our countless meetings with clients of all ages, races, religions, and education levels, we noticed common *feelings*. People seldom walked into our offices excited to get their planning done. More often, clients expressed guilt, shame and even embarrassment over not having done their planning. Highly educated neurosurgeons felt like they should have known what to do—and they don't. Even CEOs and billionaire families felt like they should have done their planning sooner. If you are feeling anything negative about being in the position you are in, don't. You are not alone. Consider the following statistics:

- 32% of people in the United States have a will
- 82% with an estate plan don't have the most needed document (Hint: it's not a will)
- 16% of Americans are confident that they are ahead of saving for retirement
- 47% of millennials invest in the stock market
- 31% of Americans' most trusted source for advice are financial firms and advisors
- 84% believe attorneys do not have high ethical standards
- 11% have strong trust in insurance agents
- 70% of wealthy Americans worry their children will use their inheritance unwisely

If you haven't done any planning or are unsure if your planning is adequate, you are in good company. If you don't know where to start or who to trust, you are obviously not alone.

EVEN THE WEALTHIEST, MOST PROMINENT FAMILIES GET BAD ADVICE

If you had told us when we started our careers that the richest people in the world get bad advice, we wouldn't have believed you. Today, after working with hundreds of millionaires, five billionaire families, the private client groups at the biggest accounting and investment banking firms, and hundreds of professionals, we aren't surprised at all. Let's examine a couple of quick examples.

- **Elvis Presley's family lost over $8 million.** Perhaps the most famous person of the twentieth century, Elvis worked with many attorneys on the countless contracts he signed for music, films, and endorsements. When he died, Presley's heirs unnecessarily lost over two-thirds of their estate to taxes and probate fees.
- **Prince made doves and heirs cry**. Decades in the music industry led Prince to distrust attorneys. Prince's estate unnecessarily went through six years of probate, costing millions of dollars in legal fees. In the end, a judge awarded each of his five half-siblings a substantial share of the $200 million estate he'd intended for his sister. A simple $3,000 trust would have eliminated all of this.
- **Dodgers' owners lost $1.8 billion.** The O'Malley family owned the baseball team from 1947 to 1997. Inadequate estate planning forced Peter O'Malley to sell the team for $311 million to Rupert Murdoch's News Corp. Fifteen years later, when the O'Malley family attempted to repurchase the Dodgers, they were outbid by Guggenheim. The purchase price of the Los Angeles Dodgers was $2.15 billion.

BEWARE CONVENTIONAL WIS-DUMB

Most people don't know where to start or how to start. As a result, they don't get their planning done. Those who do plan often make mistakes. There are many reasons for this which we will cover in the book. Dare to be different and break free from the herd. You can do something different and get way out in front of potential problems before they arise. ***giraffeMONEY Essentials*** will give you the foundation to help you know what to look for and where to focus so you can maximize your impact and minimize your effort, aggravation, and frustration.

CHAPTER 3

IT'S NOT ME, IT'S YOU—AVOID THE #1 MISTAKE

Did you know that each giraffe's fur has a unique pattern, much like humans have distinct fingerprints? Are you wondering how the authors can claim to value your time, yet still waste some of it with obscure zoological facts? We promise to weave only a few of the fourteen invaluable lessons from another of Chris' books, ***Be the Giraffe***, into this book—and when we do, they will make sense . . . eventually.

According to Maslow, love and belonging come right after survival and safety in a human being's hierarchy of needs. It makes sense to want to "fit in" and belong. The extreme opposite, not fitting in, is loneliness, seclusion, and isolation. Some people's company may inspire us to wish for solitude in small doses, but none of us want that forever. It's in our survival DNA to want to be part of *something*.

Unfortunately, this basic human need has been studied ad nauseam, and then exploited. Think about the phrase, "Keeping up with the

Joneses." It's a thing. Campaigns that lead to "I gotta have it" mentality result in irrational behavior. Consider the following:

- Parents got into fist fights at toy stores trying to buy Cabbage Patch Kids and Tickle Me Elmo (over Christmas presents for toddlers)
- Teens were literally shooting other teens to steal their Nike Air Jordans
- Perhaps most outrageously, people sacrifice $2,600 for a fanny pack with the Gucci logo on it.

This borderline psychotic behavior is very common in retail—and the foundation for the world's biggest brands. Retail is the first word in retail financial services. Consider these examples:

- People who wanted to believe they were part of a special, private club looked past all the warning signs of Bernie Madoff and Alan Stamford's Ponzi schemes, and they lost over $2 billion.
- Over 80,000 physicians and dentists were scammed into tax fraud by Donald Guess and his Xelan firm because they believed in special plans for doctors.
- Goldman Sachs was "caught" in the housing bubble controversy. They were ordered to pay over $5 billion in fines, but people still use them.

These are just a few of the more egregious examples, but billions of people make many smaller mistakes every day. How can so many people make so many bad decisions? There are four contributors:

Mainstream media is not your friend. No, we are not talking about "fake news." We are talking about "folk news." Media outlets live off advertising. Advertising rates go up as the audience grows. It should be no surprise that nearly every news station, newspaper, financial magazine, and financial website has audiences with household incomes ranging from $55,000 to $110,000. This is where the biggest audience is. The content of the programming and advertisements is directed at people with those incomes. If you have any aspirations of earning $150,000 to $1,500,000 per year, you need to lobotomize yourself of (or at least forget) everything you have read or heard on finances through these channels. They just don't apply to you and your goals.

Advice of friends and family. You should take advice from people you trust. You should not, however, assume that sharing the same zip code or the same 23andMe makes you similar. Yes, you may have the same relative income or even the same relatives, but that is not enough. For example, one of Chris' best friends in his town has a seven-figure income working for one of the country's most famous financial firms. They both have three children, share political beliefs, and have similar retirement goals. It would be reasonable to assume their financial plans might be similar, right? The author is married to a schoolteacher. His friend's wife is a doctor. That one factor completely changes their situations. There are other family dynamics to consider, like who is expecting an inheritance or who is expecting to have the financial burden of taking care of parents or in-laws.

Playing the odds. In a game of blackjack, it always makes sense to double down with an 11 when the dealer is showing a 5. You win more often than you lose, but sometimes the dealer still pulls a 21 and you lose your bet. For a $5 or even a $500 hand, that's not that big of a deal. In life, the cost of being wrong can be much more damaging—and is probably not worth the risk.

- You have a 14% chance of dying before 65 when you are 40. For a young family looking to save for their future, 86 out of 100 of them won't need life insurance or estate planning documents. What if your family is among the 14%?
- The same 40-year-old has a 21% chance of becoming disabled for 90 days or more. How long can your family support itself without your income?
- For the optimistic, the odds of winning Mega Millions are 1 in 302,600,000. Do you want to rely on that long shot to get your family out of a hole?

Relying on the advice of a *trusted* financial giant. Sure, these companies have been around for a long time. Some say you can trust they will be there in the future, but the bankruptcy of SmithBarney may change that view. Despite the billions of dollars of fines that these trusted companies have recently received for compliance indiscretions (Goldman Sachs: $5.4B; Deutsche Bank: $7.2B; BNP Paribas: $8.97B; JP Morgan Chase: $13B; and Bank of America: $30B), we are not suggesting these firms are trying to hurt you. We are suggesting that these firms are trying to *herd* you. The only way firms with thousands of employees can service millions of clients is with leverage (see Chapter 5).

To effectively deliver any service on a large scale, you must create efficiencies. This comes from simplifying the offerings and convincing large groups of people that they want what you have. McDonald's hasn't sold billions of "the best hamburgers in the world." McDonald's serves an inexpensive, mediocre, but extremely consistent product—and uses a ton of advertising to remind us of that. *Side note: Chris shares his amazing experience on a private tour of one of McDonald's three suppliers in **Be the Giraffe**. It's worth a read.*

What you get from working with large financial institutions are the Big Mac and fries of the financial world. It's likely to be consistent and mediocre, and maybe moderately priced. In the end, it will not be customized to your needs and will not offer any fancy bells and whistles, though you may be led to believe so. Your financial plan needs a lot more than a Shamrock Shake or McRib once a year.

UNDERSTANDING *YOUR PERSONAL ECONOMY*

The concept of your "personal economy" emphasizes managing finances effectively to achieve financial stability, security, and, ultimately, financial freedom and well-being on YOUR terms. It involves making informed decisions about income, expenses, savings, investments, and debt to support your current and future goals and aspirations.

Here's a quick test: assume CNBC is reporting the following stories:

- Experts fear the economy is sliding into a recession
- The S&P dropped by 20%

- The NASDAQ closed down 700 points
- Jerome Powell appeared on Capitol Hill and announced another pause in the fed funds rate

At the same time:

- A change in the tax law eliminates a large deduction your business had been taking
- Your mother was just diagnosed with Lou Gehrig's Disease, and there are little savings and no insurance coverage to pay future medical bills
- Your accountant has informed you that you failed to heed his advice about retirement plan taxes upon distributions
- You need back surgery that may prevent you from traveling for work

Which of these events really impacts your personal financial situation? If you said the first set, you may be an investment banker. For the rest of us, the second set is the obvious answer. Media has so much power over our perspectives. Millions focus on the state of financial news as the greatest factor in their personal finances, instead of on events and decisions that affect our bank accounts! Many of us succumb to the uneasiness surrounding the volatility of the market, which, in turn, makes us feel powerless to change our own personal financial situation. The outcome is a lack of action to change our circumstances or relying on advice that may or may not make sense for us. This folly leads us to one of the greatest financial planning mistakes we encounter in our practice: focusing on the macroeconomic condition of the nation rather than understanding your own personal economy.

Even though we said in the beginning of this book that time is valuable, we are going to introduce you to twenty-plus topics, hand-picked, to help you determine what makes sense for you and your family. Our intention is to eliminate the need for you to spend your precious time meeting with ten professionals across several disciplines for three or four hours each. The time you spend reading this book is designed to save you time and money in the future tracking down disjointed solutions to problems you shouldn't have to concern yourself with. This is why we think this book should cost $10,000.

CHAPTER 4

WHY THIS BOOK SHOULD COST $10,000

You have a finite amount of time and a limited amount of money. With any endeavor, you should maximize the value you receive from committing either of these resources. Whether it's our one on one consulting, group trainings, live events, or written materials, we want to add value in three ways:

1. Save time
2. Save money
3. Eliminate pain (aggravation and frustration)

SAVING YOU TIME

In the introduction, we acknowledged that your time is valuable. How valuable? If you consider that the average work year is 2,000 hours (based on working forty hours per week for fifty weeks per year). If you make $100,000 per year, your time is worth $50 per hour. If you earn $250,000 per year, your time is worth $125 per hour. If you want to earn $500,000 per year, you should think about your time being worth $250 per hour.

How much time could you possibly spend on financial planning and wealth management? According to the Bureau of Labor Statistics, in 2023, Americans spent an average of fifty-four minutes per day, or 330 hours per year, engaged in financial planning activities. Wow! If you told us it felt like you spent 330 hours getting through our book, we might believe you. That is a lot of time.

SAVING YOU MONEY

In Chris' experience lecturing on entrepreneurship at multiple universities, it's exciting to see so many young people who plan to work for themselves and become millionaires or billionaires. The problem is that they don't understand the formula for success. You can become a billionaire if you can make or save someone (or some group of people) $10 billion. It is completely reasonable to expect to retain 10% of the value you create.

In our consulting firm, we charge value-based fees. Our model is to charge 10% of the value we expect to create over some time (often two to three years). If we can save you $1,000,000, we would charge $100,000. Similarly, if we say this book should be worth $10,000, a reader should expect to find at least $100,000 in savings. ***giraffeMONEY Essentials*** can deliver this in many ways, including:

- **Time is money:** We hope this book will save you at least fifty hours of research, meetings, and worry annually. If you and your spouse value your combined time at $200 per hour, that's $10,000 per year!

- **Income taxes**: $5,000 to $10,000 per year, for the next ten to twenty-five years, could be realized from the strategies in this book. If you own a business, the amounts could be 10x that!
- **Capital gains taxes**: Structuring investments properly could save you over $100,000 in taxes on investments over a lifetime.
- **Probate fees**: One simple legal structure could save your family $100,000 or more in unnecessary probate fees.
- **Estate taxes**: An underutilized, but extremely powerful, tool could save your family $5 million in estate taxes without losing access to any of your assets.
- **Professional fees**: By focusing on strategies that pay for themselves, and eliminating expensive, time-consuming strategies that are less impactful, you should be able to save tens of thousands of dollars on professional fees. In addition, advisors in our network work all over the country. The discounts they offer readers of our book (we don't receive anything) could be worth $5,000 or more.
- **Litigation expense**: Anybody can get sued. If you own or operate a business, you can expect those odds to go up dramatically. By implementing asset-protection planning, you could discourage or

dismiss creditors and save tens, if not hundreds, of thousands of dollars (and countless hours) of litigation.

When you add up all the benefits these strategies could offer you, the number should exceed $100,000 and potentially be worth well into the millions of dollars over the rest of your lifetime.

ELIMINATING YOUR PAIN (STRESS, FRUSTRATION, AND AGGRAVATION)

It's hard to put a price on pain and frustration, but psychologists and pharmaceutical companies seem to have found a way to do it for their benefit. This book should save you pain that can be difficult to quantify.

What would each of these be worth to you?

- Knowing that your financial planning is done
- Feeling comfortable that you are on track to retire on time
- Knowing your family would be taken care of if you died prematurely
- Being confident that your advisors understand you and your goals
- Not worrying about life's changes because you know your plan is flexible
- Sleeping easily when threatened with a lawsuit because you implemented asset-protection planning with an expert

These items each have a different value to each family. We can't really put a price on them, but you can try to do so if you still aren't convinced that this book is worth the hours you will put into finishing it. If you are feeling anything other than the positive feelings bulleted above, you're not alone there either.

IT'S NOT YOUR FAULT—IT'S THE AMAZON EFFECT

Have you ever shopped for anything on Amazon? Of course you have! You probably have Prime same-day delivery, Walmart Plus, Instacart, and Grubhub on your cell phone. Heck, you even have Fiverr and TaskRabbit in case you need a picture hung or an IKEA bookshelf put together. If you want something in thirty minutes or less, you are going to get it, and if it's late it better be free! What a world we live in today, with everything we could ever want at our fingertips.

Have you ever tried to gift shop on Amazon without knowing what you are looking for? It's an absolute nightmare. Endless options and opportunities leading to paralysis by analysis. Sometimes you take a flier, and your gift becomes an even bigger surprise to you—after you see it. I once bought a statue for someone's new garden, only to see it sitting on my friend's desk as a paperweight.

This is what happens with financial planning. If you know exactly what you need, you can find an expert who does that specific thing every day. If you don't know exactly what you need (other than guidance), you can expect an endless parade of professionals who will give you everything you ever wanted, provided they are licensed to sell it.

Essentials will help you get a better handle on what you need so you can confidently move forward without worry.

CHAPTER 5

YOUR SHORTCUT TO SUCCESS—LEVERAGE

giraffeMONEY Essentials is a book about finance (albeit with lots of zoology metaphors). We need to briefly revisit high school physics to make a point. I invite you to google the word *leverage*. You will see links to the *Cambridge English Dictionary*, *Merriam-Webster*, Investopedia, and Thesaurus.com. You will find definitions of leverage as both a noun and a verb. You will find both financial and business definitions.

One of Google's four definitions states:

> **lev·er·age,** *verb:*
>
> use (something) to maximum advantage.
>
> "The organization needs to leverage its key resources."

Thesaurus.com offers a list of synonyms. We are partial to these three:

1. Influence
2. Advantage (or edge)
3. Power

If you can influence others to help you gain an advantage, you will have successfully achieved some level of power. "First, you get the money. Then, you get the power." Thank you, Tony Montana.

Leverage allows a person to be more efficient, more effective, and much more powerful. Leverage helps you get more done in less time, with less effort, and with less money. Do you know anyone who wants to spend more time and money while working even harder? If you are looking for a shortcut to financial success, leverage is the better path.

Leverage is how most of the modern world was built and how most fortunes were created.

If you've ever taken out a mortgage to buy a home or a loan to buy a car, then you have used financial leverage. While borrowing to purchase a home provides a place to live, most reasonable people expect the value of their home to appreciate over time, hopefully at a greater rate than they borrowed. If you've taken out a loan to purchase a car, that car will allow you to go to work and earn an income that is greater than the cost of your monthly payment. The loan may also allow you to buy a car that is more reliable than the beater you would have bought if you'd had to pay cash.

The way we prefer to look at leverage is to accomplish more with less of your own effort, time, and money. It is about the never-ending quest to become more efficient and effective in everything we do to build, maintain, and protect our wealth. While there are many avenues to utilize leverage, we will focus on four: money (yours), money (other people's), time, and people.

Leveraging your own money is the oldest and most basic form of leverage. It has been documented all the way back to the ancient times of nations, empires, kings, and emperors. These nations had enough money to fund expeditions to discover new lands and acquire even more wealth. A visit to any of the museums of Rome or other ancient cities will reveal examples of this leverage.

The most common way to use leverage is with other people's money (OPM) or debt. Many affluent people throughout history have achieved their wealth by borrowing at lower rates and investing the loan at higher levels of return. Many famous and infamous real-estate tycoons built their empires in just this fashion. They put down a small percentage of the total costs to build properties and used OPM to fund the remainder of the costs. By borrowing money from the bank at rates that may be as low as 6% to 10% and developing properties that may have an overall return of 15% per year, the leverage gives the investor a significant return on their investment.

Another way to leverage OPM is called equity. That is, taking someone else's money and giving them a piece of a business or investment in return. In this situation, the investor takes more risk, but also gets a higher expected return than the bank would get with debt. If you've ever purchased an individual stock, equity ETF, or mutual fund, you have been leveraged—you are the source of other people's money!

Leveraging time is one of the most important skills a person can learn. Your time is your most finite resource, and finding ways to magnify your impact for a given unit of time is the most significant way to magnify your effectiveness. Successful people identify skills in others and empower them to get things done for them. This allows the business owner to focus on the highest and best use of their time. When considering how you leverage your time, it is very important to utilize the skills, resources, and connections of your team. This leads to the final of the four.

If leveraging time is the most important thing you can do, leveraging people is how you will do it. Despite all the challenges people have with advisors, agents, attorneys, and accountants, you will need to walk with a select group of them on your path toward greater leverage, peace of mind, and financial freedom. It may be difficult to identify people you trust for each role, so leverage experts. If you've ever worked with a general contractor (GC), you may have asked them for recommendations on an electrician, landscaper, or painter. Why not do the same thing with your financial team? You may meet with your estate planning attorney a handful of times in your life, but your financial advisor and accountant will work with these professionals frequently across many clients.

Leverage their networks and enable them to "GC" your personal financial team. In ***giraffeMONEY***, we discuss how to select and maximize the advisors of your team. If you need help finding creative, honest advisors in your area, we will gladly introduce you to some we have grown to know and love over the years.

YOUR BETTER PATH

Congratulations! You have already taken steps toward "leveraging up" by reading ***giraffeMONEY Essentials***. This information will give you an advantage and influence over advisors who might be trying to take advantage of you. The power you will have in negotiation, and the confidence you will have in the process, will make money work for you—instead of the opposite.

The next six sections will teach you how to protect assets, eliminate unnecessary taxes, plan for your family, avoid financial disasters, and get more out of your investments. At the end of each section, there will be both a summary and checklist. The checklist will guide you on next steps to move that area of your planning forward. Individually, each section can have a significant impact on your wealth. Collectively, they can have a compounding effect on the long-term growth and sustainability of your wealth for generations to come. As you will see, many tools and strategies show up in multiple sections. These give you a great deal of flexibility and leverage, which is why we include them.

Are you ready to start making some serious strides down your new path toward increased wealth and peace of mind? Let's go!

SECTION 2

PROTECT CURRENT & FUTURE WEALTH

Wait! Before you skip ahead to more exciting wealth-building strategies, perhaps you remember a parent or teacher telling you, "An ounce of prevention is worth a pound of cure."

If you take a little time to protect yourself in the early stages of your planning, we promise that you will save yourself an immeasurable amount of time, aggravation, frustration, and money in the long run. On top of that, you just finished reading a section about *leverage*—getting more out of your time, effort, and investments. That is exactly what we will help you do with this section of ***giraffeMONEY Essentials***.

Even if you don't have any money to protect (yet), we will help you understand how relatively inexpensive planning will help you discourage potential lawsuits ***and*** protect you in the event something bad does happen (because the t-shirt is right: shit does happen).

More importantly, you will learn how these same tools and strategies that offer protection can also help you eliminate unnecessary income and estate taxes, create investment flexibility for your family and your business, and help you save tens of thousands of dollars in professional fees. Though risk management and legal structure may seem boring to most, the information in this chapter will pay for itself more than sixteen times over.

CHAPTER 6

WHY ASSET PROTECTION?

It is estimated that there are more than forty million lawsuits filed every year in the United States (source: Onelegal.com). Why so many? As of January 1, 2022, the American Bar Association (ABA) National Lawyer Population Survey reported a total of 1,327,010 active lawyers in the United States and its territories. They gotta make a living somehow!

IT WILL GET WORSE BEFORE IT GETS BETTER

According to Norton Rose Fulbright's 2023 Annual Litigation Trends Survey, 86% of respondents believe legal disputes will stay the same or increase. Macroeconomic factors that drive litigation include an impending recession, rising interest rates, heightened inflation, tight labor markets, and market volatility.

YOUR BETTER PATH

The American Rule, that each side must pay its own legal fees, has afforded people of all classes an opportunity to protect themselves through the courts. Unfortunately, this same rule may have had the unintended consequence of creating an overly litigious society. While many complain about the system and blame the attorneys, a more prudent and effective path is to integrate legal tools and strategies that protect your wealth into your comprehensive financial plan. When done properly, asset protection will provide retirement, estate, and investment planning benefits that will pay for itself. As always, we want to get the most leverage from our time and our money. To prioritize where to focus, let's better understand our risks and ways to mitigate them with the "Liability Ladder."

CHAPTER 7

UNDERSTAND THE "LIABILITY LADDER"

One joke about lawyers is that no matter what question you ask about the law, you will be given the same answer: "It depends." Asset protection is no different, in that it's far from an exact science. What we do know for sure is that humans are involved in every lawsuit, so human nature can't be ignored.

The liability ladder is a ten-point scale that we created to help you better understand how much risk you face with different behaviors and ownership structures.

LEVEL OF RISK FOR EACH STRUCTURE (HIGHER # IS GREATER RISK)

Level	Strategy or Solution
10	General Partnership—Operating Business
9	Sole Proprietorship—Operating Business
8	General Partnership or Sole Proprietorship—Real Estate
7	Corporate Owned Assets
6	Own Name, Spouse's Name, Joint Ownership, Living Trust
5	Limited Liability Company (LLC) or FLP
4	Irrevocable Trusts
3	Debt Shields
2	Exempt Assets under State Law
1	Exempt Assets under Federal Law

DO NOT WORRY! If you are unfamiliar with any, most, or all the items in this list, that's perfectly fine. We will help you understand what they are, and appreciate how they are different as you embrace the ***giraffeMONEY Essentials***.

This ladder, or scale, is far from perfect, but it does a nice job of measuring relative risk. For example, running a business as a general partnership (with another person) or in your own name (as a sole proprietor) could expose your personal wealth to business liability, and vice versa. This is the worst type of ownership structure and should always be avoided. Conversely, assets like retirement plans that are protected under federal law get the lowest score because they offer protection without requiring you to do anything special to receive it.

HOW TO APPROACH ASSET PROTECTION

Throughout this book, we will focus on tools and strategies that 1) may have significant impact; and 2) offer a great deal of planning flexibility. The goal of any plan should be to address the most pressing concerns with as little aggravation as necessary and as much flexibility as possible. Don't get too hung up (a scary thought for a giraffe with a long neck) on absolute or perfect protection. When you have little wealth to protect, or you face very little liability, you should be able to get plenty of benefit from a few simple techniques.

As your wealth grows, or your exposure to liability increases, you may find it necessary to go deeper and read ***giraffeMONEY: Billionaire Secrets for Millionaires*** or purchase the *Money Differently* bundle (mentioned at the back of the book). Until you have more significant wealth to protect, you should be able to reach adequate levels of protection without having to climb very high up the planning ladder.

YOUR BETTER PATH

We will show you how to protect wealth, reduce taxes, invest more wisely, avoid financial disasters, and provide for future generations. For now, the best thing you can do is make a list of the assets and structures you currently have. Use the space on the next page to write down the assets you currently possess. Later, you can fill out how best to protect these assets.

INVENTORY OF YOUR ASSETS

Asset	Name	Value	Title/Ownership
Ex 1	*Bank account*	*$12,000*	*Own Name*
Ex 2	*Home*	*$200,000*	*Jointly w/ spouse*
1			
2			
3			
4			
5			
6			
7			
8			
9			
10			
11			
12			
13			
14			

Be sure to include any assets worth more than $10,000. This may include cars, real estate, business interests, insurance policies, investments, retirement plans, homes, etc.

CHAPTER 8
ASSET PROTECTION MYTHS

Our conversations with clients are not quite as funny as "texts with teens," but we do come across some beliefs that are funny (if we can help you fix them).

Five common myths are:

1. My assets are owned jointly with my spouse, so our assets are protected.
2. My assets are owned by my spouse, so I'm safe.
3. I can just give assets away if I get into trouble.
4. My living trust, or family trust, protects my assets.
5. I have insurance, so I'm covered.

These myths can be dangerous if they lull you into a false sense of security. Let's examine each of these common myths and dispel them.

MYTH NO. 1: MY ASSETS ARE OWNED JOINTLY WITH MY SPOUSE, SO I'M OKAY.

Most people hold their homes and other property in joint ownership. Unfortunately, this ownership structure provides little asset protection. In community property states, community assets will be exposed to community debts regardless of title. Community debts include any debt that arises during marriage as the result of an act that helped the community (marital entity).

Any claims resulting from professional or personal liability, income-producing assets (rental real estate property, for example), or auto accident (by either spouse, any child living at home, or anyone driving your car) would also be included.

Even in non-community property states, joint property is at least 50% vulnerable to claims against either spouse. Titling assets with a spouse will expose between 50% and 100% of that asset to potential creditors. If this asset is of any significance (you can exclude the ten-year-old Toyota Camry you're saving for your teenager), you don't want to own it with your spouse.

MYTH NO. 2: MY ASSETS ARE OWNED BY MY SPOUSE, SO I'M SAFE.

This is one of the most common misconceptions about asset protection—and one we see implemented too often by families that have one high-risk professional spouse (like a surgeon or obstetrician). The faulty assumption is that the doctor would be sued personally for malpractice, but the assets would be safe because they are owned by the non-physician spouse.

The first part of the assumption (that the physician will be sued personally) is true. The second part about protection is false. Once creditors have a judgment, they are often able to seize assets owned by the spouse of the debtor by proving that the income or funds of the debtor were used to purchase the asset. To determine if the asset is reversible, three questions can be asked:

1. Was the vulnerable spouse's income used to purchase the asset?
2. Has the vulnerable spouse ever used the asset?
3. Does this spouse have any control over the asset?

If you answered "yes" to any of these questions, then the creditor can be paid from these assets. Given the strength and flexibility many strategies offer (you will see as you read more sections), there's no good reason to rely on this weak protection for any significant asset.

MYTH NO. 3: I CAN JUST GIVE ASSETS AWAY IF I GET INTO TROUBLE.

If this were the case, you would need only a shovel and some geocaching skills, and you could hide your treasure and play your own game of *Pokémon Go* later. All states have created laws prohibiting such fraudulent transfers. To oversimplify the statute, any asset transferred after an incident took place may be ordered by a judge to be returned to the transferor so it may satisfy the creditor's claim. What's interesting about this statute is that it doesn't matter if the creditor knew about the event or the potential for a lawsuit to be deemed a fraudulent transfer. For example, a missed diagnosis or a sponge left in a patient by a physician may not trigger a suit for months or years. Any transfer of wealth from a physician from the date of the surgery (gifts to children, for example) could be ordered to be returned.

MYTH NO. 4: MY LIVING TRUST (OR FAMILY TRUST) PROVIDES ASSET PROTECTION

Later in this section, and in greater detail in the estate planning section, we will talk about the power of trusts. What's confusing is that there are two categories of trusts—revocable trusts and irrevocable trusts.

Unsurprisingly, many consumers are confused. Revocable trusts are often referred to as family trusts, living trusts, or loving trusts. Yes, these trusts are invaluable for basic estate planning, avoidance of probate, and handling of powers of attorney; however, there is no creditor protection from these trusts until you die. We are in the business of protecting assets you can enjoy while you are alive, so we can't rely on revocable trusts for protection.

MYTH NO. 5: I HAVE INSURANCE, SO I'M COVERED.

Fun facts: Chris started his career as an actuary—making rates for insurance companies. Tony's father is the CEO of an insurance company. Both Tony and Chris own insurance agencies and have licenses in dozens of states. You could say we are "insiders" who know a bit about insurance.

Though insurance can be an inexpensive way to transfer risk, it has its limitations. Have you ever asked yourself why an insurance policy is fifty to one hundred pages (or longer)? When Chris and Tony worked at multiple insurance companies, each of them had over two hundred lawyers for one reason—to protect the company. Inside every policy are exclusions and limitations. These are the occurrences, events, and amounts that will not be covered. If you aren't careful, you may not become aware of the exclusions until after attempting to make a claim. In addition to the exclusions, there are other concerns with insurance.

- **Loss of control:** When you make a claim, you lose control of your defense. A suit against you could damage your reputation. Once you make a claim, the insurance company has the right to settle and pay.
- **Gaps in coverage:** An excellent strategy to inexpensively secure additional coverage is to buy an umbrella policy. A common mistake is to not match the underlying limits of your home and auto policies to the requirement of the umbrella policy—causing you to pay the difference.
- **Higher premiums:** Once you make a claim, your rate may increase.

YOUR BETTER PATH

Don't be concerned or alarmed if you believed any of these asset-protection myths. Don't be disappointed if the protection you thought you had looks inadequate now. With the myths dispelled, you can now focus on how to incorporate effective asset-protection into your comprehensive plan.

TAKE AN INVENTORY OF YOUR EXISTING ASSETS SO WE CAN REVIEW THESE LATER

1. What assets are owned by you personally?

2. What assets are owned by you and your spouse?

3. What assets are owned by your spouse only?

4. What assets are owned by your living trust?

5. What is your liability limit on your automobile policy?

6. What is your liability limit on your homeowners' or renters' policy?

7. What are the underlying limits of your umbrella policy?

CHAPTER 9

MAXIMIZING "FREE" PROTECTION

The essential strategy of this book is to maximize impact and flexibility while minimizing aggravation, time, and costs. In this chapter, we will explore how to maximize the value of the assets that are protected without any additional legal or accounting fees. You won't lose control of the asset, either—giving you lots of flexibility.

At the bottom of the Liability Ladder are the structures with the least amount of risk. They are often referred to as "exempt" assets because you could go so far as to file bankruptcy to get rid of creditors, and these assets would be "exempt" from the bankruptcy. In other words, you could wipe out all your debts (excluding student loans) and keep these assets after the bankruptcy.

FEDERALLY EXEMPT ASSETS

When liabilities exceed assets, individuals and corporations who feel they may never be able to meet the obligations may appeal for bankruptcy under Chapter 11 (reorganization) or Chapter 7 (liquidation). In a Chapter 7 bankruptcy, the debtor will be able to keep any assets (after the bankruptcy) that federal law deems exempt. The two significant asset classes that federal law protects are qualified retirement plans (QRPs) and individual retirement accounts (IRAs). The term "qualified retirement plan" means that the retirement plan complies with certain Department of Labor and Internal Revenue Service rules—often referred to collectively as ERISA (Employee Retirement Income Security Act). Individual retirement accounts have several technical differences, but they are now given exempt status as well.

DRAWBACKS

While this protection is unlimited, you must recognize that federal protection applies only if you have filed for bankruptcy. If you were simply sued and a creditor is trying to take the funds in your pension or IRA, bankruptcy protection would not apply. You would have to take the step of filing for bankruptcy to shield the asset. For many with professional licenses, this might be too great a cost for the protection. If you do not file for bankruptcy, the amount of value in the QRP or IRA that would be protected outside of bankruptcy would be governed by the applicable federal and state laws.

STATE EXEMPT ASSETS

In addition to federal protections, each state offers additional exemptions. There are some humorous outdated ones, like two oxen in West Virginia (look that up), but the most significant state exemptions include:

- Qualified retirement plans and individual retirement accounts
- Primary residence (or homestead)
- Life insurance
- Annuities

QUALIFIED RETIREMENT PLANS AND INDIVIDUAL RETIREMENT ACCOUNTS

Outside of bankruptcy, any protection for QRPs or IRAs is provided by state law. Most states provide a high level of protection for QRPs. Fewer states shield IRAs at a similar level. For IRAs, several states will protect only the amount reasonably necessary for support, leaving it up to a judge to decide how much should be shielded in any case. While this may be adequate for most people, it may not be adequate for those who have contributed for a long time.

PRIMARY RESIDENCE: HOMESTEAD

Your home is your castle. For many, the home is the family's most valuable asset. Though some states provide excellent protection for one's home, the reality is that state laws have not changed as home prices have soared over the last fifty years. For example, most states only protect between $10,000 and $60,000 of home equity. Make all the jokes you want about living in New Jersey—the state protects $0 of equity.

To determine how well a homestead law protects your home, you should compare the protected value in your state to the equity you have. Start by subtracting the value of any outstanding first and second mortgages from the fair market value of your home. For a rough estimate, you can look up your address on Zilllow.com and subtract your total mortgages from that estimate. If you live in a home with a $300,000 fair market value and have a $150,000 mortgage, then your equity is $150,000. If your state protects only $20,000 through its homestead law, then you still have $130,000 ($150,000 of equity minus $20,000 homestead) of exposed equity.

Homestead protection is often automatic, but may require additional action in some cases. Each state has specific requirements for claiming homestead status. In some states, you must file a declaration of homestead in a public office. Other states set a time requirement for residency before homestead protection is granted. Never assume your home is protected. If you're wrong, your inaction may cost you the protection you deserve. An asset-protection advisor can show you how to comply with the formalities in your state. If the homestead isn't sufficient for your equity, advanced techniques for protecting your home may be required.

LIFE INSURANCE: PROTECTED EVERYWHERE

All fifty states have laws protecting life insurance; however, each state offers varying amounts of protection—for the cash value and the death benefit. For example:

- Many states shield the entire policy proceeds from the creditors of the policyholder. Some also protect against the beneficiary's creditors.
- States that do not protect the entire policy proceeds do protect some proceeds.

- Many states protect the policy proceeds only if the policy beneficiaries are the policyholder's spouse, children, or other dependents.
- Some states protect a policy's cash surrender value. This means you can amass a very sizeable asset that is not restricted from being accessed before age 59½ like a retirement plan, and you can protect it without any legal fees.

In some states, insurance death benefit proceeds are great for leaving money to heirs. In other states (like Texas, Florida, New York, and others), very wealthy families put millions of dollars into policies because the cash values are protected from creditors and taxes (the topic of the next section). Throughout the tax, investment, and estate planning sections, you will learn how insurance products have even greater flexibility and additional planning benefits.

If you want to better understand how various insurance products work and learn how to navigate agents and products to give your family the most flexibility at the lowest possible cost and aggravation, you will want to read this book and perhaps dive into the deep end and read ***giraffeMONEY*** too. You could save yourself some of your valuable time and lots of disposable aggravation and contact us through our website (www.beyondwealth.pro). We will show you how to eliminate upfront expenses, avoid unnecessary commissions, and get companies to compete for your business.

ANNUITIES: SHIELDED IN MANY STATES

Annuities are insurance contracts that were designed to offer similar benefits to retirement plans and IRAs. Typically, after-tax dollars are invested into annuities to take advantage of the tax-deferred growth and compound interest. The attractiveness of annuities goes beyond the tax deferral, as the insurance company offers multiple investment options and some minimum guaranteed returns. If your underlying investments appreciate, your account increases in value. If the investments go down, annuities protect your principal—and, in some cases, offer a minimal average return over the life of your product. When you consider that annuities are protected from creditors in many states, you can see how this diverse combination of benefits makes annuities a valuable and flexible wealth-planning tool.

Caution: All annuities are not created equal. They have varying upfront charges, annual maintenance fees, and a wide range of surrender (exit) fees. You will want to work with an experienced and ethical annuity expert. If you are intrigued, Tony and his team can help you review your existing annuities or find you competitive options in less than a week.

YOUR BETTER PATH

You can see how exempt assets offer quick and easy protection. Some combination of insurance products and retirement plans will likely be part of your planning. Because you can't practically place every dollar of your wealth into exempt assets, you will have to utilize legal strategies at some point. The next chapter will introduce the most common and flexible asset protection tool—the limited liability company (or "LLC").

INVENTORY OF YOUR EXEMPT AND NON-EXEMPT ASSETS

EXEMPT ASSETS	
Name	Value (Net of Loans)
Retirement plans like 401(k), 403(b), 457	
Total Value	

POTENTIALLY-EXEMPT ASSETS	
Name	Value (Net of Loans)
Primary Residence	
IRAs & Roth IRAs	
Life Insurance Cash Values	
Annuities	
Total Value	

NON-EXEMPT ASSETS	
Name	Value (Net of Loans)
Real Estate (other than home)	
Bank Accounts	
Investment Accounts	
Business Interests	
Collectibles & Other	
Total Value	

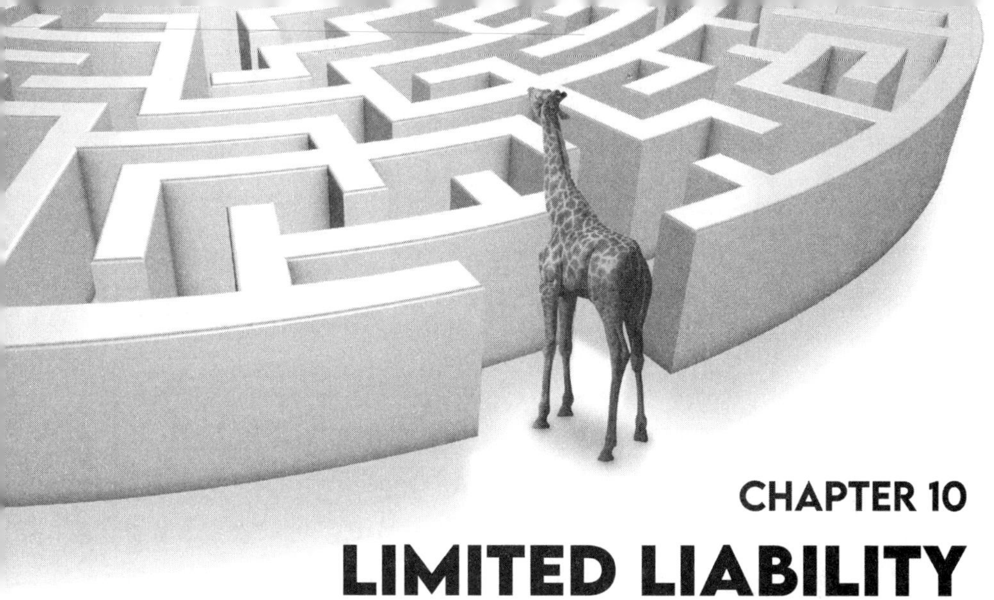

CHAPTER 10
LIMITED LIABILITY COMPANIES

While exempt assets may be the most effective asset-protection tools, most clients will need to go beyond the use of exempt assets to protect assets. Of all the legal tools we use to shield assets, the two we use most frequently are family limited partnerships (FLPs) and limited liability companies (LLCs). For simplicity, we are going to focus only on LLCs in this book. If you already have an FLP, or your state is one of the few that offers unique benefits to FLPs, you may consider these two tools interchangeable. If you are interested in understanding the nuance differences, you should go to law school. Just kidding. Not really. It's unimportant for now.

In this chapter, you will learn how LLCs protect assets, and tips to maximize the protections LLCs offer.

UNDERSTANDING LLC BASICS

The Uniform Limited Liability Company Act has been adopted at least partially by every state. Of course, there will be variations by state, but these oversimplified should help you get started.

1. Each state requires legal entities like corporations and LLCs to pay filing fees. These may range from $40 to $500 per year.
2. Entities must file annual reports with the states.
3. Depending on the tax treatment you elect (partnership, S-Corp, or C-Corp), you will submit either informational or corporate tax returns to the state and IRS.
4. You may be familiar with the idea that corporations have shares of ownership. In an LLC, we refer to "membership interests" because LLCs have members, not owners (or partners, as you have in a partnership).
5. LLCs may be managed (think governed or run) by one or more of their "members" or by a non-member manager. There is no "president" of an LLC—there is a manager. If that manager also owns an interest in the LLC, he or she may be referred to as the managing member. You can have more than one managing member.
6. There are (one or more) managing members or a manager.
7. LLCs have two levels of ownership. You may think of the active or controlling owners as managing members and the passive or non-managing owners and members. The managing members make the decisions.

8. You can split ownership and control. For example, many families create LLCs where only 1% to 10% of the total interests are managing interests, and more than 90% of the interests are non-managing. This bi-level structure of ownership allows a host of planning possibilities because clients can retain the decision-making of the LLCs, and the ultimate control of the assets held within the LLCs, while sharing membership ownership with family members—to reduce income taxes or eliminate estate taxes.
9. Beneficial and flexible tax treatment. LLCs can elect pass-through partnership taxation, meaning the LLC is not liable for income taxes. Rather, the tax liability for all income or capital gains on LLC assets passes through to the members. If adult children are in lower income tax brackets, income-sharing through an LLC may prove beneficial.
10. ASSET PROTECTION. You've waited patiently. The LLC and its members are given charging order protection. This is very valuable and worth understanding.

HOW LIMITED LIABILITY COMPANIES PROTECT ASSETS

If a personal creditor wins a judgment against you, the next step is to seize your assets to satisfy the judgment. If assets are held in your own name, jointly with a spouse, or in your revocable living trust, a judge may order you to surrender those assets.

However, if your assets are held within an LLC, it's not so easy. Under the Uniform Act provisions, a creditor of an LLC member cannot reach into the LLC and take specific LLC assets. The law generally allows for only one remedy—the charging order. No, this does not mean the judge can order you to charge the judgment to your credit card.

The charging order is a specific legal technique that is meant to preserve the viability of the legal entity, protect other members from having to pay the personal mistakes made by another member, and afford the creditor the right to access the funds owed from the judgment. It seems like the best of all worlds, but it has proven to be very useful for creditors.

When a creditor does file a charging order against an LLC, the LLC managing members are required to redirect any distributions due to the creditor member into the hands of the person or entity that filed the charging order. This is akin to garnishing wages of an employee of a corporation.

LIMITATIONS OF THE CHARGING ORDER

Unlike the garnishing of wages, which are paid every two weeks or so, distributions from an LLC are not so regular. The law is very specific. The charging order does not:

- Give creditors ability to take an LLC's voting rights.
- Allow the creditor to force LLC managing members to pay out any distributions (even if the judgment is against the sole managing member of the LLC!).

The charging order does not afford voting rights, so owners and partners remain in complete control of the assets. Despite the charging order, the managing member(s) still make all decisions—like the one to reinvest all earnings back into the LLC and not pay out distributions!

There is even a poison pill for LLCs taxed as partnerships. In the next section on taxes, you will learn that partnership-taxed entities do not pay tax. The "pass-through" taxation means that members who were entitled to the LLC's share of earnings are responsible for the tax on LLC earnings—even if they do not receive the distributions. This is referred to as "tax on phantom income" because you didn't get the money yet. Thanks to the IRS, the charging order easily backfires on creditors. When LLC managing members elect to not distribute earnings— the tax bill for phantom income will go to the creditor with the charging order even if the creditor never received any money.

TIPS FOR MAXIMIZING THE PROTECTION OF LLCS

We just explored how assets held within the LLC are protected from outside threats against any of the members. If you follow these tips, you will be on a safer path.

1. Segregate the dangerous assets from the safe ones. Dangerous assets are those that could generate liability—like rental real estate where someone could suffer a slip and fall, an airplane, or a car. Safe assets are valuable, but they do not generate liability—like a bank or investment account, insurance policy or annuity, or fine art. By separating safe assets from LLCs holding dangerous assets, we remove the exposure that could arise from inside the LLC.

If you kept all your assets together, and someone did slip and fall at the real estate location owned by the LLC, all your investment accounts inside the LLC would be unprotected.

2. Separate valuable dangerous assets from each other. In the beginning, one LLC for safe and another for dangerous assets will suffice. As the equity in the dangerous assets grows, you may want to separate them into their own LLCs. In the case of multiple rental real estate units, you may want to separate them so any liability arising from one does not threaten the value inside the other property.

Location, location, location. When possible, create any legal entity (including LLCs) in states with the best language for protection, taxation, fees, and reporting requirements. These may vary greatly, and over time, new case law and changing regulations may significantly change the landscape. You will want to work with seasoned providers who are on top of these changes.

YOUR BETTER PATH

Family limited partnerships and limited liability companies are two of the most utilized and most powerful asset-protection tools available to manage wealth. We are partial to the LLC and, at the risk of spoiling the surprise at the end of your journey through this book, the odds are very high that you will end up with at least two or three LLCs.

As you go through the book, ask yourself these three questions:

1. What dangerous assets require their own LLC?
2. What safe assets do you want to separate?
3. What businesses are you operating or investing in?

As you work through the rest of this section, the tax section, and the estate planning section, you will see how layering LLCs with different tax elections and multiple trusts will give your family lots of flexibility along with protections and tax-saving benefits.

CHAPTER 11

USING TRUSTS TO SHIELD WEALTH

Have you ever heard the saying, "You can't get blood from a stone"? Maybe you're a vegan and "you can't get blood from a turnip." In either case, the phrase means that you can only get from someone what they are able to give you.

Trusts are successful protection tools because trusts are legal entities, separate from individuals. They allow one party to put assets "in trust" for another. While inside the trust, the assets are neither the property of the person giving or of the person who will ultimately receive them. In the face of litigation or other threats, it could prove rather helpful to "not own" assets. Let's explore some basics, and then we can explore creative ways to leverage these tools for our own benefit.

TRUSTS

A trust is a legal arrangement that has three parties:

Grantor: The person who sets up the trust and transfers property into the trust. A grantor may also be called the trustor or settlor. The grantor also sets the rules by which the trust will be administered.

Trustee: The legal owner of the trust property is responsible for administering and carrying out the terms of the trust. He or she owes a fiduciary duty to the beneficiaries—an utmost duty of care that he or she will follow the terms of the trust document and manage the trust property properly. A trustee may be a person or an institution, such as a professional trust company or a bank. When there is more than one trustee, they are called co-trustees.

Beneficiary: The person (or people) who will ultimately receive the proceeds from the trust. These could be named individuals, classes of people (like children or grandchildren), organizations (like charities or universities), or any combination.

The Golden Rule of Trusts: for effective creditor protection, the grantor, trustee, and beneficiary must not all be the same person.

The grantor can be the trustee of a trust for others. The beneficiaries can be the trustees of a trust someone set up for their benefit. You can't be all three. We will explore this further later.

TRUST CLASSIFICATIONS

There are two different categories or classifications for trusts. One is about access, and the other describes timing.

Revocable vs. Irrevocable. A **revocable trust** can be changed or undone by the grantor at any time. An **irrevocable trust** is one that cannot be undone once it has been established. In the estate planning section, you will learn how revocable living trusts are necessary for any person who will die worth more than $100,000. For the most part, revocable trusts offer no protection, so we will put off discussion about these until we return to estate planning.

TIMING IS EVERYTHING

A trust may be considered an **inter vivos** trust or a **testamentary** trust. Inter vivos is a Latin phrase that means "while alive." An inter vivos trust takes effect during the grantor's lifetime.

Testamentary is an English word, meaning "given or bequeathed." A testamentary trust takes effect at the time of the grantor's death. Testamentary trusts are usually created in wills, living trusts, or other documents taking effect at death. All testamentary trusts are irrevocable once the grantor dies, but are generally revocable until that time.

Every trust will either be a revocable trust or an irrevocable trust, **and** either an inter vivos trust or a testamentary trust. A trust either has terms that can be changed (revocable) or terms that cannot be changed (irrevocable). These trusts take effect either during the grantor's lifetime (inter vivos) or at the time of the grantor's death (testamentary). For simplicity, we will assume that you want protection for your wealth, but these protections aren't worth dying for. If you are willing to die for protection, you will love the section on estate planning later.

We will focus on inter vivos irrevocable trusts when talking about asset protection!

WHY IRREVOCABLE TRUSTS PROTECT ASSETS

Once assets have been transferred into a properly structured trust (also called "funding the trust"), the assets are property of the trust. Because an irrevocable trust cannot be legally undone, there is no benefit to a creditor attempting to "step into the shoes" of a grantor creditor and attempt to reverse the transfer. Since the grantor has no rights to the assets in a trust, the creditor of the grantor cannot access those funds either.

In the case of creditors of the beneficiary, the trust also provides protection. Even though the trust assets may pay out to the beneficiaries in the future, creditors of the beneficiaries cannot force distributions from the trust. The trustee is required to manage the trust assets per the terms of the trust agreement. Leaving an inheritance in trust for children is a wonderful way to protect them from potential creditors. Even if your children are already married, you can create a trust for them that could be protected from any future divorce. This is a very easy way to get around contentious prenuptial and postnuptial agreements that can cause a lot of family discord (this is examined in greater detail in the next chapter).

THE DEVIL IS ALWAYS IN THE DETAILS

In every legal structure or strategy, there are countless details that must be managed properly to ensure that you give yourself the best chance of success in the event of any challenge. Irrevocable trusts are no exception. Here are a few tips, details, and considerations for your irrevocable trusts.

The grantor cannot reserve any power to revoke, rescind, or amend the trust or retain any rights, either directly or indirectly, to reclaim property transferred to the trust. In other words, there can be no strings attached.

1. Gifts to trusts are given the most scrutiny under fraudulent transfer laws because there is no for-value exchange as there is with contributions to a limited liability company (LLC). You want to do your planning before you have a creditor.
2. If the grantor is concerned about creditors, it might be best to not have the grantor serve as the trustee, nor allow the grantor to appoint a trustee that the courts would not consider to be at arm's length. Those who do not qualify for being at arm's length include a spouse or close relative. Even the appointment of a close friend may invite scrutiny. Courts closely examine the relationship between the grantor and the trustee to determine whether the trustee is acting as the grantor's alter ego. If there is such a relationship, courts will ignore the trust and allow creditors to reach the trust assets.

A corporate trustee, such as a bank or a trust company, is much less likely to be judged as an alter ego, thereby giving your trust an added layer of security.

TWO ESSENTIAL CLAUSES FOR AN IRREVOCABLE TRUST

There are two essential clauses that an irrevocable trust must contain for it to properly protect its assets. These clauses are not necessarily important to protect the trust creator but for shielding the beneficiaries from their creditors.

Spendthrift clause: The spendthrift clause allows the trustee to withhold income and principal, which would ordinarily be paid to the beneficiary, if the trustee feels the money could or would be wasted or seized by the beneficiary's creditors. This clause accomplishes two goals:

First, it prevents a wasteful beneficiary from spending trust funds or wasting trust assets. If you worry that money in a trust for your children would be wasted if not controlled, use a spendthrift clause. The trustee can stop payments if your child spends too quickly or unwisely.

Secondly, the spendthrift clause grants the trustee the authority to withhold payments to a beneficiary who has an outstanding creditor. The creditor only has a right to payments actually paid by the trustee. He cannot force the trustee to make disbursements.

Anti-alienation clause: The anti-alienation clause prohibits the trustee from transferring trust assets to anyone other than the beneficiary, especially creditors of the trust beneficiary. While the spendthrift clause allows the trustee to withhold payments if a creditor lurks, the anti-alienation clause goes one step further—it prohibits the trustee from paying trust income or principal to anyone but the named beneficiaries.

YOUR BETTER PATH

You don't have to embrace becoming a stone or turnip to enjoy asset protection. Trusts allow you to transform assets, or interests in assets (think non-managing LLC interest), into trust property. Since trust property is neither your property nor the property of your children or grandchildren, you can create amazing levels of protection when you use these tools.

In the estate planning section, we will show you how you and your spouse can both create irrevocable trusts for each other to create an amazing balance of protections, access, and tax avoidance.

CHAPTER 12
DIVORCE PROTECTION

MARRIAGE IS THE CHIEF CAUSE OF DIVORCE.

—GROUCHO MARX

According to the American Psychological Association, approximately 40% – 50% of first marriages end in divorce. The divorce rate for second marriages is even higher, at 60% – 67%. Besides being common, divorce can also be an emotionally devastating and financially disastrous experience.

Divorce protection is not about hiding assets from a soon-to-be ex-spouse. Good divorce planning is about creating incentives for couples to try to work things out and protecting your children and grandchildren in case things don't.

Given the statistics enumerated above, it is almost a certainty that either a child or grandchild of yours will get divorced. Assuming you don't want to create a financial incentive for someone to divorce your heirs, a little time in this chapter could go a long way.

WHY DIVORCE CAN BE A FINANCIAL NIGHTMARE

After suffering through my parents' divorce, I (Chris) swore I would never get married, never have kids, and if I did get married, I would most certainly never get divorced. It was a bad day at the ballpark as I went 0 for 4 (I've been married twice). So much for the best laid plans. My ex-wife and I were not great together, so it was no surprise that we didn't treat each other well during the divorce. Though we could have handled it better, the lawyers fanned the flames until we didn't have any money left. Then, miraculously, all issues were resolved, and our divorce was finalized.

COMMUNITY PROPERTY STATES

Nine states have community property laws: Arizona, California, Idaho, Louisiana, Nevada, New Mexico, Texas, Washington, and Wisconsin. Community property law stipulates that if there is no valid pre or post-marital agreement, the court will equally divide between the ex-spouses any property acquired during the marriage other than inheritances or gifts given directly to one spouse or the other. Even the appreciation of one spouse's separate property can be divided if the other spouse expended effort on that property during the marriage and the property appreciated.

EQUITABLE DISTRIBUTION STATES

Non-community property states are called equitable distribution states because courts in these states have total discretion to divide the property equitably or fairly. The court will consider the duration of the marriage, the age and conduct of the parties, and the current and future earning potential of each former spouse. The danger of equitable divorces is that courts often distribute both non-marital assets (those acquired before the marriage) and marital assets (those acquired during marriage) equally between the divorcees. In this way, courts often split up property in ways that the ex-spouses never wanted or anticipated.

CAN A PRENUPTIAL PROTECT YOU?

A prenuptial agreement is a written contract between the spouses. It specifies the division of property and income upon divorce. It also states the responsibilities of each party regarding their children after divorce. Finally, these agreements lay out the respective responsibilities of each partner during marriage, such as the financial support each spouse can expect, and the religious education the children will receive. The agreement cannot limit child support because the right to child support lies with the child and not the parent.

Most importantly, with a prenuptial agreement, there is much less opportunity for attorneys to spend all the marital assets arguing over every little thing—because the agreement was handled in advance. The only thing the attorneys can argue is whether the agreement is valid.

REQUIREMENTS FOR A VALID PREMARITAL AGREEMENT

Each state differs slightly on what is required for an enforceable premarital agreement. In most states, the agreement must be written, signed, and notarized. There must be a fair and accurate disclosure of assets leading into the marriage. Both partners must be represented by counsel, and the agreement can't be one-sided.

THERE MUST BE A BETTER WAY

Yes, divorce is extremely common. Of course, you want to protect your children or grandchildren from any unnecessary emotional or financial stress. Yes, prenuptial agreements can work. The bigger question is, "Are prenups worth it?"

The process of negotiating a prenuptial agreement can do temporary, or more lasting, emotional damage. For many families, the arguments over the prenup often fracture the family dynamic. Unsurprisingly, many clients who started out insisting on a prenup for their soon to be son-in-law or daughter-in-law ended up dropping it to try to save the headaches. In many cases, it was too little too late.

What if there was a way to protect your children's inheritances without causing any uneasiness or discord? Let's look back to our old friend, the irrevocable trust, for guidance.

PROTECT YOUR CHILDREN FROM DIVORCE

When your children or grandchildren come to you, giddy with exciting news about their recent engagements, the last thing they want to hear you ask is, "Are you going to sign a prenuptial agreement?" In fact, if you weren't paying for the wedding, you might lose your invitation for asking such a question.

As you learned earlier, the secret to protecting assets from divorce is keeping the assets as separate property and not commingling them with community or marital property. You can't count on your children to do this, so you are going to do it for them, without requiring the consent of your child or the future (or existing) spouse.

By leaving assets to your children's irrevocable trusts, with the appropriate spendthrift provisions, rather than to them personally, you can achieve this goal. Of course, if the children take money out of the trust and use it to buy a home or other property, that property will be subject to the rules of their state.

To illustrate this point, let's look at the example of Rob and Janelle, college sweethearts who got married right after graduation. Within a few years, their romance turned sour, and Rob could no longer handle the physical and emotional abuse. However, during their three-year marriage, Janelle received a sizable inheritance and used it to pay off the couple's home. When they filed for divorce, Rob's attorney successfully argued that his time and labor on the house, and the fact that he lived in it, except when Janelle occasionally kicked him out and he had to stay with his mother, made half of the equity in the home, or $100,000, Rob's fair share. Though Rob and all his friends will argue the $100,000 was a small consolation for what he had endured, Janelle's grandparents certainly didn't intend for Rob to receive their inheritance.

What could Janelle have done differently to ensure that she protected her assets? Her grandparents could have left her the inheritance through an irrevocable trust that only allowed her to take out so much money per year. In that case, she would have used the interest from the inheritance to pay the mortgage down each month. If she did so, the corpus of the inheritance would have remained separate property and would not have been part of the divorce settlement.

In the three short years of their marriage, they would have had nearly zero equity in their home and Rob would have left the marriage with the property that he brought into it, and his wounded pride—but none of Janelle's grandparents' life savings.

YOUR BETTER PATH

In a nutshell, a little proactive financial planning can go a long way to making sure that a divorce doesn't completely disrupt a family's financial situation. It should be easy to understand why so few people are wealthy. So far, this section has shown you how family wealth can be lost to personal and professional lawsuits, disability, and divorce.

Luckily, you also learned in the last section that there are many ways to protect wealth from all those threats. There is one threat that we failed to address in this section. That is the largest threat of all: taxes. The entirety of Section 3 focuses on ways to address tax liabilities.

Taxes are such a substantial threat to family wealth that there is an additional section, Section 4, solely dedicated to estate taxes.

ASSET PROTECTION SUMMARY

We hope you walk away from Section 2 feeling like you just spent two hours in a dojo learning self-defense. The giraffe has a big vulnerable neck, but those long legs pack a hell of a kick, too. Working on your agility will help you protect yourself and your family from threats and liabilities. Whether it's lawsuits, divorce, irresponsible children, or adults who act like children, misinformation that is mistaken for conventional wisdom is a serious threat. This section is CliffsNotes for eliminating unnecessary concerns.

1. **An Ounce of Prevention**: The earlier you take proactive measures to safeguard your wealth, the less they will cost and the more likely they will be to protect you.
2. **Take It Seriously:** Shielding your wealth isn't just for the ultra-rich. In a lawsuit-crazy world, asset protection is your financial Xanax.
3. **Climb the Ladder One Rung at a Time:** Different ownership structures expose us to a wide range of risks. Strategies offer varying amounts of protection. More complicated and expensive solutions are only necessary for high-risk, high-value assets.
4. **Free Is for Me:** Federal and state laws protect assets for us—what a country! Retirement plans, some home equity, and some insurance cash values are protected. Know the laws in your state so you can get something for nothing.

5. **Myth Busters:** Joint accounts with your spouse and traditional insurance are not enough to protect wealth. Plan ahead to ensure you don't accidentally disinherit family members while trying to protect yourself.
6. **LLCs, A Better Path:** An ultra-flexible and powerful tool can reduce income and estate taxes, too. You're gonna love this one.
7. **Trusts, Your Financial Guardians**: Trusts are powerful, versatile tools for preserving assets and providing guidance for your financial legacy.
8. **Divorce-Proofing Your Wealth**: Protecting your wealth from divorce isn't just about your marriage. The divorce of children or grandchildren can unravel a legacy built over a lifetime. The right tools can remove hard conversations and safeguard your family's future.

ASSET PROTECTION CHECKLIST

	Evaluate Current Financial Situation
	Make a list of all assets, liabilities, income, and expenses.
	Identify areas of vulnerability and potential risk in your life.

	Consult Professionals
	Seek advice from legal, financial, and tax professionals
	Periodically review and update planning when circumstances or laws change.

	Set Financial Goals
	Determine short-term and long term financial objectives.
	Consider desired level of asset protection and risk tolerance.

	Insurance Coverage
	Review existing insurance policies (life, health, auto, homeowners, liability).
	Consider additional or umbrella insurance policies for extra protection.

	Legal Structures
	Establish trusts, LLCs, or corporations to separate personal and business assets
	Create wills, trusts, and powers of attorney.
	Designate beneficiaries for assets.

	Asset Protection Trusts
	Consider SLATs or IDITs in favorable jurisdictions.
	Understand the legal requirements and implications of such trusts.

	Titling and Ownership
	Review how assets are titled and owned to minimize exposure to liabilities.
	Review joint ownership, tenancy by entirety, and alternative forms of ownership with asset protection benefits (like LLCs and trusts).

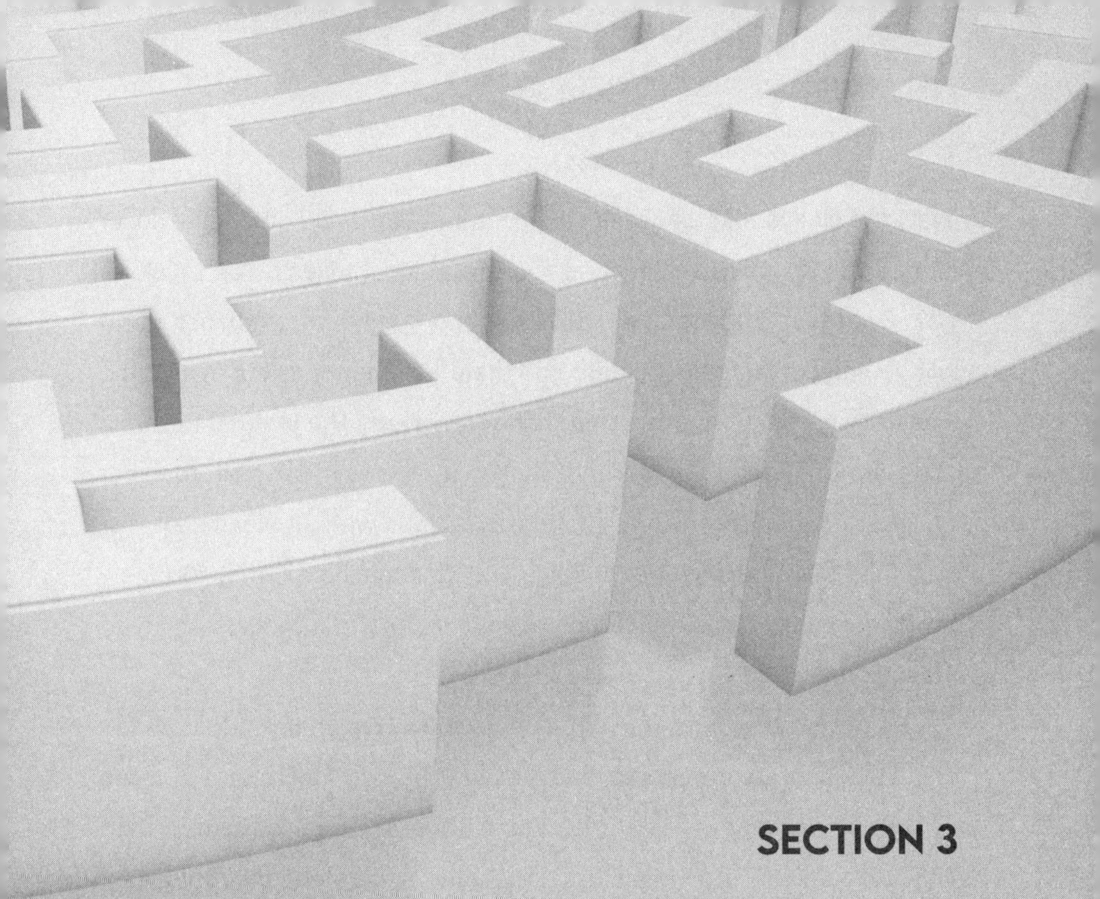

SECTION 3

REDUCE UNNECESSARY TAXES

You don't have to make a lot of money to want to legally pay less in taxes. Judge Learned Hand famously said, "No American is required to pay more tax than the law would allow. . .there is not even a patriotic duty to do so." The biggest difference between the ultra-high net worth and everyone else is that the wealthy understand that every additional dollar earned will be eroded by federal, state, and local taxes by as much as 50%. They also know that up to 50% of the family's after-tax net worth will be subject to federal estate and state inheritance taxes every time wealth transfers from one generation to the next. The Internal Revenue Code is structured in a way that makes it almost impossible to accumulate wealth and pass it to future generations without significant friction; therefore, the secret to building and maintaining a family fortune—building wealthy families—can be directly related to a family's ability to manage taxes.

Do not expect to be able to manage your taxes until you first understand taxes. Everyone should read the next chapter, "Uncle Sam's Pieces of Your Pie," to learn exactly which taxes threaten wealth accumulation and how they do so. This will help you better understand the motivation for, and benefits of, the strategies explained in the subsequent chapters.

These tools may help you reduce, defer, or even eliminate some of your tax burden while providing you, your family, or your business with additional financial benefits.

By learning and implementing the techniques in this section, you can expect to reduce unnecessary taxes and build a fortune much more quickly. This is essential to achieving greater levels of affluence.

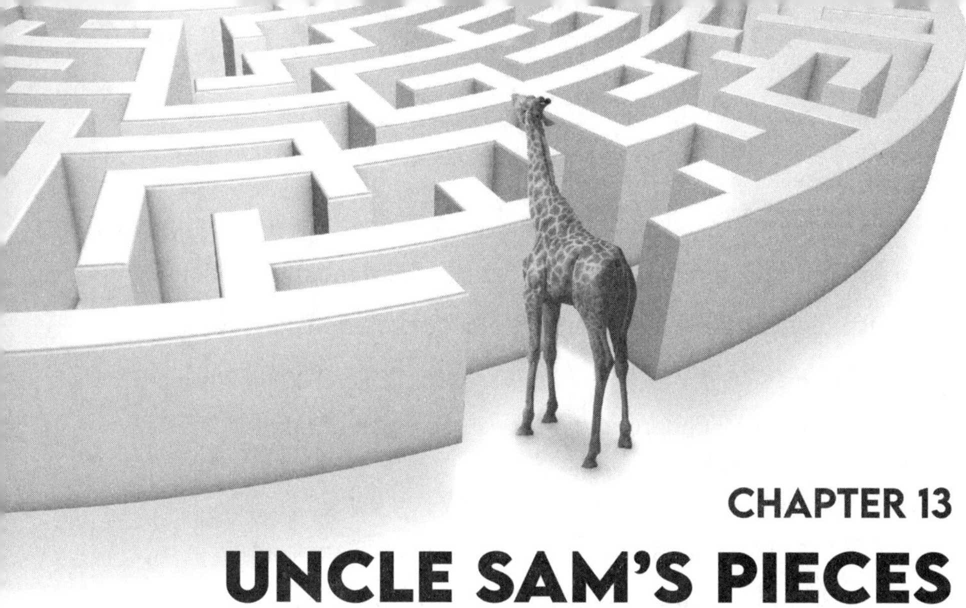

CHAPTER 13

UNCLE SAM'S PIECES OF YOUR PIE

You can't expect to successfully overcome any challenge until you fully understand what lies before you. In this chapter, we will explain the largest expense of your life—taxes. More importantly, we will share techniques to successfully reduce unnecessary taxes on earnings, investments, and generational transfers.

Is it any surprise that a mathematician's career and international credibility were built by saving clients hundreds of thousands to hundreds of millions of dollars in unnecessary taxes? No matter how many accountants, tax attorneys, or financial advisors you have, the challenges we shared at the beginning of the book always result in gaps in personal or business tax planning.

We are so confident in the inefficiencies and conflicts of interest of the different disciplines that we promise our clients to save them more in taxes than we charge—or we refund our fees. We don't say that to impress you or offer it as a shameless plug. Rather, we want to impress upon you that the complexity of the tax code and most practitioners' inability to clearly explain it to clients is a huge problem—for you!

Before we can show you how to save more of your hard-earned wealth, let's start by understanding the three types of taxes:

- Income taxes (taxes on money you earn)
- Capital gains taxes (taxes on your investments)
- Estate taxes (taxes on money you transfer)

INCOME TAXES

Every U.S. taxpayer is required to pay income taxes on all earned income. In the case of U.S. citizens, this can be from salaries or fees earned anywhere in the world. Do you know how income taxes are computed? Most people believe that they move from one tax bracket to a higher one, increasing the percentage they pay on each dollar earned. The truth is that every individual pays 10% tax on the first $10,275 of income (or on the first $20,550 for married couples filing jointly). As your income crosses into the next tax bracket, only the dollars earned within that bracket are taxed at the higher rate.

2023 Tax Brackets for Single Filers and Married Couples Filing Jointly		
Rate	For Unmarried Individuals	For Married Individuals Filing Joint Returns
10%	$0 to $11,000	$0 to $22,000
12%	$11,000 to $44,725	$22,001 to $89,450
22%	$44,726 to $95,375	$89,451 to $190,750
24%	$95,376 to $182,100	$190,751 to $364,200
32%	$182,101 to $231,250	$364,201 to $462,500
35%	$231,251 to $578,125	$462,500 to $693,750
37%	$578,126 or more	$693,751 or more

Source: Internal Revenue Service.

To better understand how income tax is computed for families, let's look at the example of Mike and Gina. Mike and Gina are married and file their taxes jointly. Gina earns $240,000 per year as a software engineer, while Mike runs an in-home business that generates $10,000 per year in income. For simplicity, the table above assumes they have no deductions, and they live in a state with 0% state income tax. Based on their $250,000 of total adjusted gross income, their federal income tax liabilities are $40,152.

Marginal Tax Bracket: 24%

Effective Tax Rate: 18.06%

If we assume they spend $12,000 per month on living expenses and save the rest, their cashflow would be:

Gross Income:	$250,000
Income Tax:	$40,152
After-tax Income:	$209,548
Expenses:	$144,000
Savings:	$65,548

Highest Marginal Federal Income Tax Rates			
Year	Rate	Year	Rate
1920	73.0%	1980	70.0%
1930	25.0%	2000	39.6%
1940	81.0%	2008	35.0%
1950	91.0%	2011	39.6%
1960	91.0%	2014	43.4%*
1970	71.0%	2022	40.8%*

***Note: For individual earners over $200,000 and households filing jointly over $250,000, there is an additional Medicare tax of 0.9% (3.8% total) in addition to federal income taxes.**

If you believe that history tends to repeat itself, or that lawmakers lack creativity, then you know what this table means. Tax rates are currently at an historical low and will likely rise, possibly significantly, in the future. We can expect this now more than ever given the stimulus spending that occurred during the COVID-19 pandemic. Could the largest U.S.

deficit in history lead to higher rates? Are you willing to bet your hard-earned money that rates will not increase again?

Back to the example of our happily married couple who filed jointly—Gina and Mike. Let's say that Gina and Mike invest $70,000 of savings into a 5% money market account. This generates a $3,500 interest payment annually. They must add this $3,500 to their income. Because they are in a 24% marginal tax bracket, the additional federal income tax liability will be $840. The $3,500 growth will only really be worth $2,660 to them after taxes (a real 3.8% return, instead of the 5% they thought they were getting).

TAXES ON INVESTMENTS

Once you earn money and pay income taxes, you aren't done with tax payments. This is only the tip of the tax iceberg. You may spend the money you earn (after taxes) on small items and pay sales tax, or you may buy real estate and pay annual property taxes.

Another possibility is that you save the money and invest it. Common investment choices include savings accounts, certificates of deposit (CDs), money market funds, stocks, bonds, mutual funds, cash value insurance policies, and real estate. A discussion of investments is offered in Section 6.

Most investments can generally be classified as either income or growth vehicles. Income investments are those that offer some type of regular return (income) to the investor. Your bank accounts, CDs, and money market funds give you an interest payment each year.

If you own traditional bonds, you receive a coupon every six or twelve months. If you own rental real estate, you may collect rental income. All these interest payments, bond coupon payments, and rent checks are added to your income for the purpose of calculating taxable income as discussed above. If you are in a 24% marginal income tax bracket, as are Mike and Gina, then you will have to pay 24% tax on those payments. If you are in a 35% marginal tax bracket, then you will pay 35% of the investment gain in taxes on that investment income. Of course, if you are not in an income-tax-free state (most are not), you could pay up to 13.3% in additional state income taxes as well.

Not all investors require immediate income from investments. Higher earners may not need current income from investments. They can afford to invest in riskier investments while looking for greater long-term appreciation. Some look for growth in vehicles such as stocks (usually small cap or technology types), hedge funds, private equity, start-ups, mutual funds, and life insurance contracts that may have any of these vehicles as underlying investments. These investments and growth vehicles are further discussed in Section 6.

If you later sell your investment for a profit, you are responsible for taxes on your realized (sold) capital gains. For tax purposes, capital gains can be categorized as long-term or short-term. Short-term is defined as realized (sold) appreciation of an asset that you owned for less than one year. If you have a short-term gain, it is treated like income and taxed at your marginal tax rate. In Mike and Gina's case, their short-term capital gains would be taxed at 24% (plus any applicable state income taxes). Of course, if their combined earned income and investment income reach $364,200, then each additional dollar will be taxed at 32%.

If you hold an asset for 366 days or more, the government gives you a benefit. You can pay long-term capital gains tax rates on your realized appreciation. Currently, these rates are 10% of the growth (for individuals who are in the lowest tax bracket) and 20% for all other taxpayers (plus applicable state taxes). This benefit gives an incentive to investors to keep their funds in one place. This stability is much better for the overall economy relative to constant buying and selling, which could significantly disrupt business. For high income earners, there is also a 3.8% Medicare tax that could bring this long-term capital gains tax rate up to 23.8%, plus applicable state taxes. This tax incentive also acts as a deterrent to potentially unethical short-term trading.

BEWARE: CAPITAL GAINS TAXES ARE AT ALL-TIME LOWS

Capital gains tax rates, like ordinary income tax rates, are near the lowest point in the history of the U.S. capital gains tax.

Top Federal Capital Gains Tax Rate			
Year	Highest Federal Capital Gains Tax Rate	Year	Highest Federal Capital Gains Tax Rate
1940	30.0%	1990	28.0%
1942-1967	25.0%	2000	20.0%
1970	32.3%	2010	15.0%
1977	39.9%	2013	20.0%

Note: For couples earning over $250,000 (or individuals earning more than $200,000), there is an additional 3.8% Medicare tax that will be added to capital gains tax rates.

Tax rates are obviously low, but there is no assurance they will stay that way. If you understand that the probability of an increase in the capital gains tax rate could be great, you appreciate the value of protecting investment gains from taxes.

Is Uncle Sam's triple dip enough? No, it isn't. After you pay your income taxes, sales taxes for your purchases, property taxes on real estate, and taxes on all your investment gains, there is still more tax to be paid.

ESTATE TAXES

When you die, Uncle Sam has an estate tax for those of you who might be worth more than $5 million at the time of death (assuming you live until at least 2026). That $5 million may include the combined value of your home, retirement plans, real estate, brokerage accounts, and insurance policies. While the rates might be between 40% (2022) and 55% (recent past), for estimation purposes we will assume the estate tax rate to be about 50% for ease of calculations throughout the section. That means that half of what you think you will leave your children could go to taxes. For a complete description of the estate tax, how it works, why the supposed repeal is a fairy tale, and how to avoid the unnecessary costs associated with it, please read Section 4.

DOUBLE (OR IS IT QUINTUPLE?) JEOPARDY—THE 70% TAX TRAP

Lastly, there is a combination of taxes that severely threatens those of you who hope to be worth more than $5 million and who might die with a retirement plan or an individual retirement account (IRA) you would like to leave your children. There is something called income in respect of a decedent (IRD).

IRD refers to the taxation of income earned by a deceased person who didn't pay tax on the income before passing away (or hadn't received the money before death to generate the tax). These income items include unpaid salaries, bonuses, and commissions, as well as qualified retirement plans (such as pensions and 401[k]s), roll-over IRAs, and variable annuity appreciation. Statistically, the qualified retirement plan and IRA balances are by far the most significant IRD assets.

YOUR BETTER PATH

It may seem crazy that there are so many ways that you can lose your wealth to taxes. Death by a thousand (repealed tax) cuts? In the beginning of the book, we talked about the complexities and inefficiencies of our laws, regulatory bodies, and professional accreditation. Our tax laws are among the most complex systems of rules ever created. We will never master them all. The best we can hope to do is attempt to mitigate our risks as we navigate our way through the fog of the system.

If you are feeling a little frustrated, angry, or even sick, we understand. Take a deep breath. The purpose of this book is to first shed light on an issue, then to help you find quick and relatively painless ways to address them. The rest of this section will focus on ways to reduce taxes on income and capital gains. Then, the entire next section is dedicated to estate planning.

CHAPTER 14

USE RETIREMENT PLANS

If you see a long history of tax benefits being afforded to a particular behavior or asset, this is generally because Congress believes that the behavior or asset provides some economic benefit to society. We will revisit these types of tax benefits for home ownership, and ownership of real estate, and cash value life insurance (CVLI) later in this section and in Section 6. In the case of retirement vehicles, the theory is that by encouraging people to fund their own retirement, the government—and the rest of us taxpayers—will not have to support them in retirement.

Two retirement tactics include:

- Maximizing available qualified retirement plan contributions for all members of the family.
- Maximizing investments in vehicles that are like qualified plans for all members of the family.

To succeed, we must leverage assets, capital, and advisors. By creating separate business entities to manage real estate and liquid assets, we can create employment opportunities for members of their families.

By creating income opportunities for family members, we can accomplish three things:

1. They generate effective wealth transfers to junior generations.
2. They create opportunities for family members to make tax-deductible contributions to their own retirement plans.
3. They may have the opportunity to use the tax advantage of blended tax rates between company owners.

MAXIMIZING THE USE OF QUALIFIED PLANS

Because tax-deductible retirement plan contributions are limited for each person, having additional family members earning income within a family business offers a wealthy family multiple tax-deductible contributions. This technique reduces the total tax liability for the family.

In Section 2, you learned that qualified retirement plans are generally afforded the highest level of protection from creditors. The use of multiple contributions also affords wealthy families a greater level of asset protection for their total wealth as more money will be invested into this exempt asset class. In addition to a reduction in current taxes and increased family savings, this strategy helps protect those savings from lawsuits. All these benefits are integral for a long-term, sustainable path to affluence.

There are many types of tax-deductible retirement vehicles. They fall into one of two categories: defined contribution plans or defined benefit plans.

Defined contribution plans restrict the amount (contribution) you can make to the plans on an annual basis. These include all forms of individual retirement accounts (IRAs), profit-sharing plans, money purchase plans, 401(k) plans, 403(b) plans, and others.

Defined benefit plans restrict how much money can be contributed to the plan at any time. The broader category, defined benefit plans, includes fully insured defined benefit plans, which are also known as 412(e)3 plans. Typically, defined benefit plans are used to help older individuals catch up on lost opportunities to make contributions.

The choice and implementation of the right plan for the situation will be determined by your planning team. The benefits of that planning will vary widely depending on each family's circumstances and the ages and salaries of the employees.

MAXIMIZE THE USE OF VEHICLES SIMILAR TO QUALIFIED PLANS

Another tactic is to use tools and techniques that mirror many of the benefits of retirement plans. Because retirement plan contributions are limited and the annual contribution amounts are based on the retirement needs of average Americans, the affluent need to utilize alternative saving and investment methods to meet their significantly higher long-term retirement needs. A common strategy to enhance long-term retirement income and reduce taxes on investment gains is to invest in cash value life insurance.

ROTH CONTRIBUTIONS: THE NEW(EST) KID ON THE BLOCK

Step by step, we will help you hang tough and retire in style. When the federal government passed the Taxpayer Relief Act of 1997, they introduced a new way to invest into retirement accounts beginning January 1, 1998. This vehicle, which was originally proposed as IRA Plus in 1989, allows taxpayers to pay taxes on their contributions when they are originally made and never have to pay taxes on these funds again. This creates a very compelling tax-management opportunity. The first downside to the Roth IRA, however, is that there is a maximum contribution amount, much like a traditional IRA. The second, unsurprisingly, is that high earners cannot contribute. That limit in 2023 is $228,000 for couples and $153,000 for single taxpayers.

Enter the Roth 401(k), the Roth IRA's younger, more muscular sibling. On January 1, 2006, investors received the opportunity to make Roth contributions to their employer-sponsored 401(k) plans. While Roth IRAs have their benefits and limitations, Roth 401(k)s allow anyone, regardless of income, to invest for retirement. Limitations on Roth contributions to 401(k)s are governed by the same contribution limits as traditional contributions.

Note: With the passing of the SECURE 2.0 act in 2022, there will be a Roth option available for many of the other types of defined contribution plans over the next several years.

YOUR BETTER PATH

Retirement plans are a great way to achieve a high level of asset protection, while reducing current tax liabilities. With the growing number of options in the qualified plan marketplace, we have the luxury to choose how and when we want to pay taxes on our qualified plan assets. By choosing to pay taxes now, you eliminate the risk of rising tax rates. With an all-access pass to your retirement funds, you don't need to worry about the tax law changes that could ambush you during retirement—when you have less opportunity to earn additional funds to make up the difference.

Further, if you have any interest in creating wealth for future generations, leveraging these new tools for your children or grandchildren could help avoid today's gift taxes, all future income and capital gains taxes, and any future estate taxes. Seldom is there something that is a no-brainer strategy in finance, but the Roth situation is a "must see" for you to discuss with a savvy advisor.

CHAPTER 15

BORROWING LOWER TAX RATES

In the previous chapter, you learned that by creating income opportunities for family members, families can increase their total capacity for tax-deductible retirement contributions. By shifting the ownership of income-producing assets to family members in lower marginal income tax brackets, wealthy families have been able to reduce total family income taxes even further.

HOW AN LLC CAN REDUCE TAXES

In addition to the creditor protection benefits discussed in the last section, LLCs offer the potential for tax- and estate planning benefits. When used properly, LLCs can save between tens of thousands and hundreds of thousands of dollars in taxes each year. In the next section on estate planning, you will learn the power of gifting (non-managing) interests of an LLC to remove wealth from your taxable estate (without giving up control). This savvy move will also help you before you die.

When you gift interests of your LLC to family members who are in lower marginal income tax brackets, they are taxed on their percentage of the income generated within the LLC. While the exact rules are more complex, children over the age of eighteen (or over twenty-four if a full-time student and a dependent) are taxed at their marginal rate. Let's see how this works by reading the case study of Danny and Rebecca.

CASE STUDY: DANNY AND REBECCA'S LLC REDUCES INCOME TAXES

Danny and Rebecca had annual taxable income of $100,000 from their rental real estate, which was worth $1 million. In a 40% combined state and federal tax bracket, their total tax on this income came to $40,000. They set up an LLC to own the real estate.

Danny and Rebecca appointed themselves as managing members, so they retained 100% control. They gifted a 3% membership interest to each of their four children (Kobe, Elgin, Earvin, and Jerry), removing a total of 12% from the estate. Because each child's interest would be valued at about $20,000 (3% of $1 million, less the minority valuation discount), no gift tax applied to the transfers to the children. Danny and Rebecca made these 12% transfers to their children annually for five years.

Under the LLC agreement, the children were taxed on their share of the LLC's income. After five years, the kids owned 60% of the LLC's interests. When the LLC earned $100,000, 60% of that income was taxed at the children's rate—15%. Their tax bill for the operation of the LLC was $16,000 (40% on $40,000, the parents' share) plus $9,000 (15% on $60,000, the children's share). How much did this strategy save them?

- Total tax with the LLC, year five: $25,000
- Total tax without the LLC, year five: $40,000
- Year five family income tax savings: $15,000

Bear in mind that there were also savings in years one through four. Additionally, under the LLC agreement, the managing members did not have to distribute any LLC income to the members. This was totally within the discretion of Danny and Rebecca as managing members. Thus, Danny and Rebecca could pay all LLC taxes with the income and reinvest the remaining proceeds.

USE TAX-EFFCIENT INVESTMENTS FOR GREATER LEVERAGE

Tax-efficient investments are used to build wealth and protect assets. In the beginning of this section, you learned that taxes on investment gains could significantly stunt long-term appreciation. You also learned that taxes on investment gains in states with income taxes could be as high as 52% of the short-term growth and 33% of the long-term growth.

The Rule of 72 states that 72 divided by the annual after-tax rate of return of an investment will give you the number of years it takes an investment to double in value.

Under the Rule of 72, an investment that returns 9% per year doubles in value every eight years. In twenty-four years, a $100,000 investment that grew by 9% per year would be worth $800,000. What would happen if this investor paid less attention to taxes? Would it make that much of a difference? Let's see.

A $100,000 investment with a 6% return would take twelve years to double in value (because 33% of the 9% pre-tax gain was eroded by taxes). At the end of twenty-four years, this investment would be worth $400,000. If your investments lose 33% of the return to taxes, you could end up with half as much money in your investment account at the end of twenty-four years. Half is a significant reduction indeed. The possibility of doubling your savings is reason enough to pay attention to taxes on your investments now.

Successful investors have always focused on after-tax investment returns. After all, a 100% return that you must pay 100% tax on leaves you right back where you started. Sometimes, tax management means investing in vehicles that are tax-exempt. Other times, it means hiring advisors who take a more active role in managing taxes. It can also mean investing to generate losses to offset gains.

C HOW TO MANAGE YOUR TAXES WITH A CORPORATION

Corporations generally elect between S (flow-through) and C (corporate) taxation. LLCs generally elect one of three types of taxation: partnership, S-Corp, or C-Corp. Partnerships and S corporations are often referred to as "pass-through entities" because they file informational tax returns. The owners (or partners or members) are then allocated their share of the tax from the pass-through entity (something taxed as a partnership or S corporation).

Corporations that elect "C" status for taxation must file corporate tax returns and pay corporate tax. Currently, the highest marginal federal corporate income tax bracket is 21%. Any dividends to shareholders will then be taxed to the individuals. This is where the term "double taxation" comes from—the corporation pays taxes, and the owners pay taxes on distributions.

It is almost universally accepted that double taxation is a bad thing. Let us be the first to tell you that, once again, conventional wisdom is not correct for the wealthy. With federal corporate tax rates topping out at 21%, there is a wonderful arbitrage opportunity for business owners with successful LLCs.

Let's assume that our business owner is fortunate enough to be in the top marginal income tax bracket of 37%. At this level, there will also be 3.8% Medicare tax, bringing the total tax to 40.8%. That means every $100 of income generated from an LLC will result in taxes due of $40.80 (whether the funds are distributed from the LLC or not!). One hundred dollars earned in a pass-through entity would only be worth $59.20 after taxes.

If $100 has been earned by a C-Corp, a 21% tax would be due, leaving $79 after taxes. Let's assume those $79 are later treated as qualifying dividends to the shareholders—or the corporation is closed (and the owners pay long-term capital gains tax rates on the gains in the entity). In either case, the $79 would be subject to a maximum tax rate of 20%. Even if we still have the 3.8% Medicare tax, 23.8% of $79 is $18.80 of tax. After paying "double tax," the $100 originally earned is still worth $60.20. When you do the math, you can see that your "double tax" results in you paying 1% less in taxes.

In the beginning of the book, we poked fun at people who "major in minor things." We are not suggesting that you spend a lot of time and money trying to save 1% on $100,000. The big win here is not the 1% savings. In the C-Corp structure, your family gets to use the extra $19 of savings in year one, and for years to come, without having to pay taxes. To put that into perspective, consider this question:

> If the IRS let you defer half of your taxes for five years at 0% interest, would you?

Of course you would! By using a C corporation, successful businesses can reduce their current tax liabilities, use the funds for new projects, and generate all kinds of benefits for their families. This is a tip many super wealthy families utilize—and the kind of idea we cover in greater detail in ***giraffeMONEY***. It's too powerful not to mention it here.

YOUR BETTER PATH

You have learned that retirement plans are excellent tools for saving money, deferring taxes, and helping you save. You also learned some amazing benefits of Roth IRAs that will give you an opportunity for "tax diversification."

In Section 2, you learned that LLCs are our favorite asset-protection tools. In this chapter, you learned that these same tools allow you to share income with family members in lower tax brackets to reduce the overall family tax burden. In Section 4, you will learn how these tools can be valuable in estate planning as well. This is a great example of flexibility—using one tool to accomplish many different things.

By creating your own corporation, you can both borrow lower corporate tax rates to grow your company faster and sponsor retirement plans for family members who may not have retirement plans available to them elsewhere.

CHAPTER 16

PRESERVING INVESTMENT GAINS

Earlier in this section, you learned that short-term investment gains can be taxed at combined federal, state, and Medicare rates of 25%, or even up to 50% or more. You also learned the Rule of 72, which is a shortcut to figuring out how fast money compounds. Consider this quick math as motivation to read this powerful section.

- If investments grow at 8%, they double every nine years.
- With 25% tax, 6% growth results in doubling every 12 years.
- With 50% tax, 4% growth results in doubling every 18 years.

If all this math is boring you, wait until you see the effect of taxes on dollars you invest for 36 years.

What happens when a $25,000 investment grows at 8% for 36 years?

- It doubled four times, $25,000 x 16 = $400,000
- If taxed at 25% each year, it doubles three times.
  $25,000 x 8 = $200,000
- If taxed at 50% each year, it doubles two times.
  $25,000 x 4 = $100,000

While the above case is extreme, it should point out that neglecting the taxation on your investment gains could have a very substantial effect on the value of your assets over a long time. In this chapter, we will touch on five ways to protect your investments from capital gains taxes: tax-free exchanges, Roth accounts, insurance, 529 plans, and charitable planning.

TAX-FREE EXCHANGES

Did you know that investors can defer taxes on some gains if they quickly "reinvest" the proceeds? Internal Revenue Codes Section 731 and Section 735 specify that, under certain circumstances, investors can exchange like property for like property and defer payment of capital gains tax indefinitely.

In the case of investment real estate, taxpayers utilizing a 1031 exchange have forty-five days from the sale to identify a possible replacement property, and 180 days from the sale of the original property to close on the replacement.

In the case of annuity and life insurance products, similar deferral rules are covered under Section 735. You may transfer the accumulated cash value in one contract into a like contract without triggering a taxable event. A life insurance policy owner may even exchange the cash value in their life insurance policy for an annuity if their need for life insurance no longer applies. It is very common for families who previously purchased whole life or indexed universal life policies to supplement retirement to "exchange" the cash values for much higher death benefit products, and larger inheritances, once they realize they no longer need the policy cash values for income.

ROTH ACCOUNTS

The hallmark of high-level planning is efficiency. Roths fit that bill, addressing multiple needs for clients. If you are willing to forego the tax deduction of a traditional retirement plan, you can pay taxes now, eliminate any risk of future tax hikes, and never pay taxes on these funds again.

We have yet to meet a wealthy client who doesn't see the value of paying taxes in advance, thereby eliminating any chance for the government to come back and get another bite at the apple. The only problem with Roths is eligibility. Everybody who takes the time to understand them wants one (or more). In 2024, individuals making over $161,000 and married couples making over $240,000 are not allowed to directly contribute to Roth IRAs.

Though many are prohibited from contributing to Roths for themselves, the "better path" you are looking for is still out there. Some business owners employ their children so they can make the $7,000 annual contribution. Investors can also perform something called a Roth conversion.

A conversion allows investors to take funds that are held in a traditional IRA or a traditional 401(k) and convert them into a Roth account.

There are currently no limitations on earned income or amount converted, allowing individuals who are in higher income brackets to get the amazing Roth benefits as well.

Perhaps you've read Chris' bestselling book ***Be the Giraffe*** and have decided to set out on your own and start your own business. In the early years, most businesses post a loss (that is, they spend more money than they earn). In your first full year as an entrepreneur, you may want to make your Roth conversion of a previous 401(k) or IRA and use the losses in your early-stage startup to wipe out some or all the taxes on your conversion.

If you were fortunate enough to sell a company, or unfortunately in a position where you had to take time off to deal with a health or family issue, you had a year when you worked less. During any year where you are in a lower income tax bracket, you may want to consider doing a Roth conversion and eliminating all those future taxes.

HIDDEN VALUE OF INSURANCE PRODUCTS

We have already learned that we can exchange the cash value of one life insurance contract for another without paying capital gains tax but this impressive little tax tool has another trick up its sleeve. By leveraging the tax-deferred accumulation of cash value in a life insurance policy, we can grow our wealth without incurring tax—much like a retirement account. But the true hidden value of life insurance is that account balance values can be accessed tax-free at any time.

When you take funds out of a retirement plan (pension or individual retirement account (IRA)), these withdrawals are always subject to ordinary income tax and may be subject to a penalty (an additional 10%

as of 2023) if withdrawn before age 59½. With a CVLI policy, you can always withdraw your premiums tax-free. You can also take tax-free loans against the growth of the cash value. There is never a tax penalty and there is no tax on the loan if you keep the policy in force and the policy is not a modified endowment contract (MEC). When the insured eventually passes, the tax-free death benefit is first applied to pay off the loans taken against the cash value of the policy, and the remainder goes to the policy beneficiaries.

We have several clients who invest more than $1 million per year into life insurance contracts. We also have many clients who invest hundreds of thousands of dollars every year into life insurance policies. These clients have some interest in the death benefit, but they are primarily interested in the wealth accumulation benefits of life insurance.

529 PLANS

For decades now, higher education has been viewed as a general requirement for individual success. Surprisingly enough, some of the most successful people in the world today are college dropouts. Herein lies the crux to the 529 conundrum.

The funds in a 529 plan grow on a tax-free basis. Because annual capital gains and dividends are not taxed in the 529 plan, the account balance has the potential to grow faster than if invested in comparable taxable investments. One of the benefits of a 529 plan is that the contributing party retains control of the assets in the plan for both investments and distributions.

If you make your annual contributions, don't mind the risk of the stock market, and don't die while you're funding the plan, the 529 plan is a much better alternative than just saving money in your brokerage account with the intention of cashing it out to pay education bills later; however, there is no guarantee that your children will go to college or graduate. In the past, this created a great deal of hesitancy as 529 plan funds may only be used for education expenses; however, starting in 2024, families can roll unused 529 plan funds to a Roth IRA for the account's named beneficiary without triggering income taxes or penalties, if the 529 plan has been open for at least fifteen years. This new technique provides family members with the ability to seed younger generations' retirement accounts whether they pursue advanced degrees or not.

CHARITABLE PLANNING

If you have a charitable intent and want to reduce current income taxes, capital gains taxes, or even estate taxes, then you should seriously consider charitable planning techniques. Often, you and your family will stand to benefit as much as the charity itself. The right team of advisors can help you understand the costs and benefits of charitable planning and manage all the complex issues.

But hiring the appropriate team of advisors cannot be stressed highly enough when considering your charitable giving plan. While taking advantage of charitable planning provides numerous tax benefits, there are still several drawbacks to most charity plans.

1. Legal Fees—Appropriate charitable planning often requires the use of trust structures. Common examples include charitable remainder trusts and charitable lead trusts. The implementation and

management of these trusts can come with substantial legal fees that last the lifetime of the trust.

2. Loss of Control—In order to take full advantage of advanced giving strategies, we must often give up control of assets we give or intend to give at a future date. This loss of control may not suit every charitably minded person's needs.
3. Complications Abound—Complexities of legal structures aside, there are other factors that contribute to the complexity of charitable planning. A prime example of this are the IRS' charitable giving rules. If a gift is given to a public charity, you can deduct the amount of the gift from your adjusted gross income (AGI) up to a maximum of 50% of your AGI. If the gift exceeds this amount, you can apply the excess as deductions against future years' income for five years. If the gift is to a private charity, then you can only deduct a maximum of 30% of your AGI, but this also can be applied forward five years.

Navigating what assets to gift, how to gift them, and to whom they should be gifted to optimize your giving strategy can appear to be a daunting task. But there are some generally accepted guidelines that we recommend you keep in mind:

1. Give assets with significant growth potential to younger generations—they will likely have a lower value now than in the future.

2. Give income-producing assets to older beneficiaries—they are more likely to need sources of current income in their advanced age and they will likely require less active management.
3. Assets that have already accrued large unrealized capital gains should be gifted to charity—they will provide the most tax advantages to the giver.
4. If you give a gift that has an unrealized loss, that unrealized loss will be gone forever.
5. Be mindful of lookback provisions when giving highly appreciated assets near death—the IRS has lookback provisions that could "pull" the asset back into your estate for tax purposes.
6. The gift of tuition made directly to an educational institution does not incur any gift tax treatment! So, give Timmy's college tuition directly to the college, not to Timmy first (he'll probably blow it on something else, anyway).
7. Payment of medical expenses made directly to the medical provider also receives the same treatment as education tuition.

YOUR BETTER PATH

Roth IRAs are the only thing that, by statute, are easy to implement and highly effective at navigating the capital gains landscape. But, as impactful as Roth IRAs are, the IRS has made them harder to take advantage of by placing income restraints on them. As a result, families that earn more than the maximum allowable income for Roth IRA contributions will seek out and employ Roth-like strategies such as cash value life insurance, 529 plans, tax-free exchanges, and charitable giving strategies to replicate different aspects of the benefits inherent to the Roth IRA.

CHAPTER 17
IS YOUR TAX ADVISOR HELPING OR HURTING?

Are you happy with the amount of personal or corporate taxes that you pay? If you said yes, we would be shocked you are still reading. If you said no, you are like every client who calls us, attends our live events, or comes to our offices.

We aren't suggesting that there shouldn't be any taxes to live in this country. We are suggesting that it is very likely that you are not taking advantage of the legal tax-planning strategies that are available to you. If you read our motivational and transformational books, ***Be the Giraffe*** and ***Go Wild***, you are familiar with the philosophy that we must take 100% responsibility for our situations in life. This chapter is going to arm you with the information you need to understand so that you can take control of your own tax planning.

YOU'RE LOOKING IN THE WRONG PLACE

Where should you get your tax advice? Most people believe their accountant is the best place to look. This is a very common mistake, as most accountants are tax preparers—adept at filing tax returns, usually for large numbers of clients. Success as a tax preparer requires the ability to manage large volumes of work at a few specific times of the year, often with some seasonal labor to assist with the rush (like retail hiring extra people before the holidays).

Within accounting, there are many subspecialties: financial accounting, managerial accounting, tax accounting, auditing, cost accounting, forensic accounting, government accounting, nonprofit accounting, international accounting, and environmental accounting. What are the odds that your tax preparer worked for a big firm long enough to become an expert in tax accounting and has expertise working with clients at income levels you hope to achieve?

In contrast, tax planning is the ongoing process of exploring a client's unique situation and integrating various strategies into their planning. This requires intimate knowledge of the client's business and a working knowledge of multiple advanced planning strategies to consider. These areas for advanced planning may include:

- Portfolio management strategies (tax-loss harvesting, private placement life insurance)
- Charitable giving strategies (donor-advised funds, qualified charitable donations)
- Estate planning strategies (lifetime giving, trust planning)

- Business planning (employer-sponsored retirement plan, asset depreciation, corporate structure, business succession, tax arbitrage, qualified opportunity zones, and more)
- Income strategies (income tax minimization, retirement plan contributions, withholding optimization, corporate management companies)
- Retirement saving and withdrawal strategies (Roth conversions, backdoor Roth IRAs, and more)

A qualified tax advisor will help minimize your tax liabilities, help optimize how you allocate your earnings and investments, maximize your deductions, and apply relevant tax credits.

WHAT HAPPENS WHEN YOU BRING IDEAS TO YOUR ADVISORS

If you had already done fantastic tax planning, you wouldn't be reading this far. We assume you are still looking for better ways to manage taxes. Have you ever brought tax-saving ideas to your advisors? How did they respond?

1. Admit their lack of knowledge and refer you to another expert. This would be a good sign!
2. Try to quickly get up to speed on the issue (on your dime). I wouldn't want a surgeon learning a procedure by working on me.
3. Simply reject the idea by stating, "The IRS doesn't like those," or "That will bring you unwanted attention." A mentor of ours once asked an audience,

"How many of you feel like your accountant works for the IRS instead of for you?" The easiest way to avoid an audit is to overpay, or max pay, the taxes for your income.

4. Get defensive. Perhaps they ask, "Who gave you this idea?" or, "What are his qualifications?" Unfortunately, many advisors struggle with their wealthiest clients. This is the Peter Principle: we rise to the level of our incompetency. Most professionals will not admit when they are dealing with issues outside their expertise.

Perhaps you have heard the phrase, "What you do speaks so loudly, I cannot hear what you are saying." Sometimes it isn't what someone says, but rather what he does (or doesn't do) that tells you all you need to know.

YOUR BETTER PATH

There is no one question to ask to be able to tell if you have a competent tax advisor for your specific situation. What you are looking for is someone who brings YOU ideas. You will want to work with someone who has a great deal of experience working with clients wealthier than you. You want a creative thinker who can handle complex planning. You want someone who is not overwhelmed with the volume of a large practice that serves many clients who are much smaller than you.

We are not suggesting that you immediately abandon your current CPA or tax attorney. We are suggesting that you take an active role in your tax and estate planning, bring new solutions to your advisors, and bring in new professionals to assist your advisors in a coordinated team approach. Because you are the client who will ultimately pay for the planning (or lack of it) that is put into place by your advisors, it behooves you to make sure your planning fits your needs and goals.

TAX SUMMARY

Taxes may not be your favorite topic, but they are one of the most important components to protecting and growing your wealth. We hope you feel a little wiser about the importance of understanding, managing, and legally minimizing tax liabilities to elevate your future. Let's review some of the keys to savvy tax planning:

- **Income Tax Basics:** Everyone pays income taxes on what they earn, and how much you pay depends on how much you make. In the US, our tax system works in brackets, so not every dollar gets taxed at the same rate.
- **Tax-Advantaged Strategies:** The wealthy have mastered the art of using the tax code to their advantage. By using retirement plans and Roth IRAs, and by engaging in charitable giving, you can significantly impact your tax burden. This will give you greater control over growing and transferring your wealth across generations.
- **Planning for the End:** No one likes to think about the end, but a little bit of planning now can save

your family and business partners a lot of pain and money down the road. By using the right combination of trusts and legal entities, you can remove the mess many leave behind.

- **Using LLCs and Corporations for Tax Efficiency:** LLCs and corporations can reduce taxes on investment gains and operating income. By understanding and applying the principles of tax-efficient business structures, individuals can achieve greater asset protection and tax savings. By shifting income to family members in lower tax brackets, you can reduce your overall tax bill. Think of it as a tax-saving family affair.
- **Preserve Investment Gains:** Investments are one of your tickets to growing and preserving wealth. Protecting investment gains from capital gains taxes is critical for long-term wealth accumulation. Strategies such as tax-free exchanges, investments in tax-efficient vehicles like Roth accounts, cash value life insurance, and leveraging 529 plans for education savings put you in the driver's seat.
- **Find the Right Tax Advisor:** Not all heroes wear capes—some wield calculators and pocket protectors. A good tax advisor is worth their weight in gold, but finding the right one can be tricky. Your advisor should be knowledgeable, attentive, and

willing to fight for every hard-earned penny while keeping you on the right side of the law.

- **Be Proactive:** Staying informed about tax laws is boring, even for accountants. It is critical to participate in the tax-planning process, challenge assumptions, and consider second opinions to ensure that strategies align with your goals and Uncle Sam's big book of rules.

Navigating the complex world of taxes might seem daunting, but with the right knowledge, advisors, and strategies, you're well on your way to keeping more of your pie. After all, it's not about how much you make, but how much you keep.

TAX-PLANNING CHECKLIST

	Consult with a Tax Professional to ensure compliance with tax laws and optimize tax planning strategies.
	Gather Income Documents: Collect W-2s, 1099s, and other income documents to accurately report all sources of income.
	Maximize Deductible Expenses such as mortgage interest, property taxes, charitable contributions, and unreimbursed business expenses.
	Maximize Contributions to Retirement Accounts like 401(k)s, IRAs, or self-employed retirement plans to reduce taxable income.
	Consider Health Savings Accounts (HSAs) and Flexible Spending Accounts (FSAs) for medical expenses.
	Review Investment Gains and Losses to control capital gains tax implications, considering tax-loss harvesting if applicable.
	Determine Eligibility for Tax Credits like the Earned Income Tax Credit, Child Tax Credit, education credits, or energy efficiency credits.
	Plan for Estimated Taxes if self-employed or expecting significant additional income and pay estimated taxes quarterly to avoid penalties.
	Review Business Expenses for potential deductions and consider entity structure for optimal tax treatment.
	Explore Tax-Efficient Investments to minimize tax liabilities on investment income.
	Consider Timing of Income and Expenses to minimize tax liabilities.

SECTION 4

BUILDING GENERATIONAL WEALTH

Estate planning is important to short-term financial stability and long-term wealth building for any family. After all, aren't you working hard to make money for your family and reading ***giraffeMONEY Essentials*** to learn how to better grow and protect that money for you and your family?

State and federal governments have complicated laws and multiple administrative offices to administer how individuals, their families, and their wealth are handled. You have a choice. You can save yourself a lot of time and aggravation and ignore estate planning altogether, trusting that the government's plans will be adequate for your heirs and future generations. Or you can make a sacrifice of your own time and money and make estate planning a priority. You will not see much of this benefit, but a relatively small commitment on your part could help your family avoid unnecessary taxes, untimely delays, significant administrative fees, and painful arguments and disagreements that will undoubtedly result from letting people who don't know your family make decisions on their behalf.

In this section, you will learn the costly mistakes over 90% of Americans make, the two tools that solve all the estate planning problems for 99% of us, and even a few clever ideas you can use to elevate your family wealth to greater heights.

CHAPTER 18

GOD, COUNTRY, FAMILY—WHICH CAN YOU CONTROL?

Congress established a federal estate tax in 1916 and has imposed varying tax rates on different estate sizes ever since. Since 2001, effective estate planning has been subject to tremendous uncertainty and change.

Estate taxes were scheduled to be repealed over a ten-year period because of the passage of the so-called Bush Tax Cuts in 2001, however, the permanency of those changes required ratification by a future Congress. For a variety of reasons (e.g., the terrorist attacks of 9/11, Hurricane Katrina, wars in Afghanistan and Iraq, the change in control of Congress in 2006, and the economic downturn beginning in 2007), permanent repeal never occurred.

It is true in a limited sense that Congress repealed the estate tax as part of the 2001 Tax Relief Act. For anyone who died in 2010—and only in 2010—the estate tax was indeed repealed for that year only.

THE GOVERNMENT GIVETH. . .AND TAKETH AWAY

At the end of 2012, three important changes occurred. First, the estate-tax exemption was dramatically increased. Second, portability was made permanent and became a huge potential estate-tax planning tool. Third, at the same time Congress was easing estate-tax rates and increasing the applicable credits against the tax, they were simultaneously increasing income tax rates and reducing the benefits of itemized deductions and personal exemptions. In other words, estate taxes became a significantly smaller issue for most Americans while income taxes became a much bigger issue, especially for individuals inheriting appreciated assets.

WHAT'S NEXT?

When Congress passed this legislation, the budget office was projecting multi-trillion-dollar surpluses in the federal government. This was back in the spring of 2001, before the economy began to falter, before the destruction of September 11, 2001, and before the prolonged military battle with terrorism at home and abroad. In 2007, the U.S. had the largest budget deficit in the history of the country, and it has only increased since then.

The Great Recession that began in 2008 caused the federal deficit to continue to increase. Fourteen years later, the effects of the COVID pandemic and rising inflation are putting additional strain on the economy, increasing the likelihood of various types of tax increases.

Because of our ongoing spending with our local challenges and our anticipated shortfalls in the Medicare system (as 30,000 baby boomers retire every day and start drawing on the funds), it seems likely that new sources of tax income will be a necessity for the federal government.

YOUR BETTER PATH

There have been three major sets of tax law changes with respect to gift and estate-tax law between 2001 and 2022. New taxes have emerged at the state level and for capital gains that fill the tax void left by a repeal. Thus, if you truly want to see that your estate passes on to your family, you must implement an estate plan and not rely on government tax agencies. At the time of this printing, we honestly have no idea what is going to change or how it is going to change.

CHAPTER 19

FOLLOWING THE HERD IS A DISASTER

Even *after* the scare of the COVID-19 pandemic, only 33% of Americans have done any end-of-life planning (source: Caring.com). This means that 67% of people don't even have a will. Of the 33% that have done some planning, three-quarters of them (25% of all Americans) only have a will for their estate planning. In this chapter, we will review the:

- costs of not having a will
- costs of having only a will
- disastrous consequences of owning any assets jointly with spouse or child
- one simple legal tool that will solve all these problems

If you consider that horrible estate planning mistakes are made by at least 7 out of 8 (92%) Americans, how can you be anything but disappointed with the government, estate planning attorneys, and financial planners?

Let's get this one tool in place for ourselves, our parents, our in-laws, and our siblings so we can avoid lots of unnecessary aggravation, frustration, fees, and taxes.

DO YOU WANT THE GOVERNMENT WILL?

If you die without any will, this is known as dying "intestate." When this happens, you receive the universal will that your state government has created for everyone in the state. Though the rules vary among the fifty states, they are formulaic and very rigid, with little room for interpretation. Usually, your nearest relatives receive your property at the state-allotted share for that class (spouse, children, parents, siblings). Your friends, cousins, or favorite charities will receive nothing. There are no adjustments for siblings or children, even if some are estranged or if some are in a better financial situation and don't need the money. In many situations, the "formula" hurts the surviving spouse, leaving funds that could have supported the widow or widower to adult children or others.

Finally, if you have minor children and you and your spouse die without a will, the courts then decide who will become the legal guardian of your children. What parent would want a judge to decide who will care for surviving children?

WHERE THERE'S A WILL, THERE'S A PAY(MENT)

Whether you have the government's will or your own will, you still have another hurdle to clear. In every state, the will must go through probate. The literal meaning of the word probate is "to prove or validate." In legal textbooks, probate is defined as the process by which a court legally recognizes a death and authorizes the management and distribution of the estate.

THE PITFALLS OF PROBATE

Delays: Probate often takes between one and two years to complete in many states, and the more states you add into the mix, the longer it can take. During that time, your beneficiaries must wait for any inheritance. Perhaps worse, the representatives of your estate may have to petition the court for permission to conduct any transactions involving your estate assets during this time. This process could make it difficult to sell estate property or invest estate assets during the probate process.

Costs: Probate can cost between 3% and 8% of your probate estate, or the value of your entire property passing under the will. This pays the courts, the lawyers, appraisers, and your executor (the person in charge of handling your affairs during this process), among others. In some states, these probate fees are paid on your gross estate—not considering any mortgages on your assets. In these states, if you die owning $1 million worth of assets that have mortgages of $800,000, your estate will pay probate fees based on the $1 million market value of your estate, or approximately $50,000. This is money that could have gone to your beneficiaries rather than to the courts and lawyers.

Privacy: Probate is a public process in all states. Anyone interested in your estate can find out who inherits under your will, how much he or she inherits, the beneficiaries' addresses, and more. While you may not be famous or worry about the newspapers exploiting this information, think of your beneficiaries—your surviving family members.

They certainly will not appreciate the many "advisors" calling them with hot tips. These charlatans find beneficiaries by examining probate records. They know who they are and how much found money they must invest.

What seems fair to some may seem completely unfair to others. This is definitely the case with privacy and probate. Probate is designed to make sure that all potential beneficiaries are given an opportunity to review the will and make objections. For this reason, the will has to be public.

When you die, it could take a very long time just to track down all potential beneficiaries (especially if they live abroad) to give them notice. Not only will your intended heirs have to wait a very long time, but they may also lose a significant part of an inheritance to people you haven't spoken to in decades. Even if the probate process does distribute your assets to the people you intended, they still must pay the costs of administering this process.

Control: In probate, the courts control the timing and final say-so on whether your will, and the wishes expressed therein, are followed. Your family must follow the court orders and pay for the process as well. This can be expensive and frustrating.

Double probate: If you own real estate outside of your state of residence, your will must be probated again (in an ancillary proceeding) in each state where real property is located.

Example: The Cobbler's Dad Had No Shoes (That the Son Could Find)

When Chris' dad, Ray, passed away (April of 2020—in the midst of the pandemic), we couldn't find his will. His father's lawyer had retired, and the office was closed. The will proved impossible to track down. Probate created unnecessary legal costs in the thousands of dollars.

Even though Ray had only two living children and no spouse, and a seemingly simple plan for his estate, the sale of his condo was held up for almost a year as the estate cleared probate. For larger estates, especially those that hold business interests or property in multiple states, probate can cost 6% – 8% of the total value of all assets. This doesn't include the cost of delays in making important business decisions or the costs of making additional mortgage or rent payments on assets you otherwise would have sold.

Chris' dad's estate was easy. In the event of multiple marriages, children from previous marriages, or a non-spouse significant other, the probate of a will may result in expensive and lengthy court battles by family members contesting the division of assets.

EASY WAY TO AVOID PROBATE—JOINT OWNERSHIP

The most common way for married couples to own real estate and bank accounts is to own them jointly. This avoids probate, as any asset that is jointly owned passes directly to the other owner "outside the will." Though this may seem to be a useful way to avoid the delays and costs of probate, it creates other problems.

THE DANGERS OF JOINT OWNERSHIP

In the eyes of the law, this automatic transfer takes effect the instant you die. Your will or living trust (described later) will have no effect on jointly held property. If you designated certain beneficiaries in a will or trust to receive your share of jointly held property, they will be disinherited, and the surviving joint owner(s) will take it. This avoidable tragedy occurs every day, especially in situations where one child is taking care of a parent. Consider these stories:

William, a man in his late 60s, marries for the second time. Shortly after the wedding, he puts all his significant property—his home, his winter vacation condominium, and his stock portfolio—into joint ownership with his new wife. Within six months, William dies. The home, the condo, and the stocks all go to William's new wife. His three children and eight grandchildren inherited virtually nothing, even though William had made ample provisions for them in his will.

Susan's will bequeaths her property equally to her son and daughter. Because her son lives near her and he pays her bills, Susan put her house, her safe deposit box, and her bank account in joint ownership with him. When she dies, Susan's son will get all the money in the bank account and safe deposit box, as well as the house, regardless of the provisions of the will. Unless the son is extremely generous, the daughter will get close to nothing.

Cecilia, a single mother in her 30s, has an eight-year-old daughter, Debbie. Cecilia has invested some of her excess income in buying old multifamily homes, which she and her partner fix up and rent to tenants. If she dies before they resell the properties, her partner will own the properties, leaving nothing for her daughter.

THE NEED FOR A WILL AND A LIVING TRUST—AND *NOT* JOINT OWNERSHIP

Advisors recommend combining a living trust with a short will called a pour-over will. A living trust is a legal document that provides direction for the use of your assets (and body) at the time of your death. A living trust is a revocable trust, meaning you can change it at any time. During your lifetime, the assets transferred to the trust are managed and controlled by you, the trustee, just as if you owned them in your own name. When you die, these trust assets pass to whomever you designated in the trust, automatically, outside of the probate process. Other benefits of the living trust include:

- Avoiding the unintentional disinheritance caused by joint tenancy or joint ownership (this happens in most second marriages).
- Preventing court control of assets if you become incapacitated.
- Protecting dependents with special needs.
- Providing for guardians of children if you are incapacitated (but still alive).

FUNDING THE TRUST

The transfer of assets to the living trust is also known as funding the trust. If you create a trust and don't fund the trust with assets, it is completely ineffective. If the asset has a registration or deed, change the name on the document from John Doe to "John Doe, Trustee of John Doe Revocable Living Trust." If the asset is jewelry or artwork that has no official ownership record, use an assignment document to officially transfer ownership to your living trust.

As sole trustee of the trust, you have the same power to buy, sell, mortgage, invest, and so on, as you did before. Because the trust is revocable, you can always change beneficiaries, remove or add assets, or even cancel your trust entirely. When something does change, the trust offers great benefits:

When you die or become disabled, your successor trustee will take over. These duties involve collecting income or benefits due to your estate, paying your remaining debts, making sure the proper tax returns are filed, and distributing your assets according to the trust instructions. This person or entity acts like an executor for a will; however, unlike a will, actions under a living trust's direction are private and are not generally subject to court interference.

The living trust allows you to decide when your beneficiaries receive their inheritances, instead of having a court decide. You may want this to be immediate, over time, or at some point in the future. You decide how the trustee distributes assets.

CASE STUDY: THE BRONSON FAMILY

Steven Bronson, 62, was otherwise healthy when he passed away in October of 2020. Steven's eight children, from two marriages, were understandably heartbroken—and unaware of how successful their father had been. Steven had built an impressive $15 million commercial real estate portfolio. Steven was also an astute investor, with an excellent track record of trading options. Unfortunately, his estate plan was on a shaky foundation with only a will.

Because Steven's LLCs owned properties across seven states with numerous limited liability companies, the estate had to clear probate in all seven states before funds could be released. Unfortunately, Steven had several speculative positions with his stock and options portfolio. Prior to his passing, Steven traded these accounts weekly—benefitting from market shifts. Because there was no clear plan for taking over and managing the accounts, no trades could be made.

Three years later, the family has paid hundreds of thousands of dollars in legal fees and lost millions of dollars in Steven's "frozen" investment accounts—and probate is still not complete. The saddest part of this story is that a $5,000 legal tool could have eliminated the delays and another five to ten thousand dollars of planning could have eliminated all fees, taxes, and delays. This story is more common than you might think.

YOUR BETTER PATH

Talking about death is not easy for many people. Unfortunately, over 90% of people fail to have the simple combination of a living trust and pour-over will that can solve so many problems for most American families. As you will see in the rest of this chapter, there are two or three other strategies that will take care of more than 90% of future taxes and fees for 99.9% of the population. The living trust is such a strong foundation for building an efficient and effective estate plan. Make sure you get yours done, or reviewed, as soon as possible.

CHAPTER 20

HAVING YOUR CAKE AND EATING IT, TOO

From an estate tax perspective, there has always been a dilemma. Each spouse has a unified credit. This is the amount that a spouse can leave to heirs (during one's lifetime or at death) without federal estate taxes. In 2024, that amount is $13,610,000 per person. The problem has always been that the exemption is not portable. That means that, although you can leave an unlimited amount of wealth to your spouse without tax, you do not transfer your "get out of taxes free" card along with the assets. This creates additional planning difficulties.

Alternatively, there has always been an array of techniques to move money from a taxable estate down to the next generation. Though outside the scope of this book, ***giraffeMONEY Essentials*** shows you ways to remove $50 million to $250 million out of a taxable estate with very little friction. Removing large estate values is not the problem. The challenge was always that the success of these techniques was predicated on the irrevocable transfer to the next generation. It used to be very difficult for one spouse to retain access and nearly impossible for both spouses to have access to the money. The "reflection" of the wealth between spouses or from one generation to another was simply nonexistent.

TIMING IS EVERYTHING

A client owns a very large national company. During that short window when there was amazing estate planning leverage, they were able to move 99% of their net worth out of their estate through a strategy like the one you will see in this chapter. Now, fewer than ten years later, they have a company worth almost $100,000,000 and a taxable estate of significantly less than $5 million. They took advantage of the situation, and you should, too.

THE INCREDIBLE SHRINKING GIRAFFE?

Considering the potential for major tax law change, you must consider creating a Spousal Lifetime Access Trust ("SLAT") as soon as possible. By creating his and hers SLATs and gifting assets to those SLATs, you can fully utilize your $27,220,000 of combined gift tax exemptions. Even if you are not worth $27 million, you would utilize the SLAT for as much as you do have. How can I say this with such conviction? See for yourself.

DESCRIPTION OF HIS AND HERS SLAT STRATEGY

- A SLAT is an irrevocable trust. The assets are not subject to any of your creditors.
- Assets transferred to the SLAT, and their appreciation from the time you transfer them until you die, should not be subject to estate taxes when you die.

- The assets of the SLAT should not be subject to creditor or divorce claims of any of your beneficiaries—like children or grandchildren.
- A SLAT is designed to receive gifts from you or to borrow funds from you to make investments on behalf of your descendants. The Trustee (who can be your spouse) will use the trust assets for the benefit of the beneficiaries during their lifetimes.

More than 7 Years of GOOD LUCK—This Mirror Isn't Breaking.

- Your Spouse May be a Beneficiary of SLAT. Depending on the assets transferred to the SLAT, your spouse may be a beneficiary of the SLAT for your children. Your spouse may also serve as the trustee or Co-Trustee of the SLAT, controlling assets he/she may also use for health, education, maintenance, and support in the accustomed manner of living.
- Spouses May Create Similar SLATs. In addition to a SLAT established for the benefit of your spouse and descendants, your spouse may create a similar SLAT for the benefit of you and your descendants and fund this SLAT with her remaining gift tax exemption.
- Many clients prefer to establish two SLATs (one for each spouse). This structure allows each spouse access to the assets of his or her respective SLAT while providing the other benefits explained in this chapter.

POTENTIAL RISKS OF USING A SLAT

The amazing attorneys we work with to implement very impactful strategies are adamant that clients understand every possible risk. We appreciate this about them, so we agreed to share the four risks they insist clients be aware of while contemplating this and any other estate planning technique. Below the risks, we have added a list of the practical impacts and the workarounds we use to easily mitigate each of these risks.

A SLAT is an irrevocable trust, and as such, any gift to it cannot be undone.

Reality 1: You aren't losing anything. If you and your spouse split up your community property, and give it to each other's SLAT, you two collectively still have control and access to all your assets.

Reality 2: There isn't much inconvenience or cost to this irrevocable gift.

Divorce. Gifts you make to the SLAT for your spouse, or your children cannot be reacquired.

Reality 1: If you and your spouse held your assets jointly and did not implement this strategy, the court would divvy up your assets in a divorce.

Reality 2: A future divorce would be much less contentious and less expensive because the assets would already have been separated and gifted.

Death. When your spouse dies, the trust you created for your spouse, children, and grandchildren would become for the benefit of the children (or other named remainder beneficiaries). You would not have access to that half of your assets.

Reality 1: This one is real. You may need to have access to more than half of the estate to cover your living expenses, but it is easily managed.

Reality 2: To hedge against this risk and to provide additional liquidity for the surviving spouse, life insurance is often purchased on each spouse. You would hold life insurance on your spouse in the trust you can access. Your spouse would own a policy on you in the trust she can access. This easily eliminates this problem.

Reciprocal Trusts. We must be careful to create trusts that do not violate the "reciprocal trust" doctrine which would negate some of the benefits.

Reality 1: Trusts must not be exact mirror images of one another and must have differences that would allow the IRS to determine that your economic positions were different before and after the gifts.

Reality 2: This is easily managed by seasoned attorneys. I work with such attorneys who are licensed to work in at least 40 states. If you would like a referral, please contact me at www.chrisjarvis.com/contact.

HOW ONE FAMILY TURNED $34,000 INTO $74,000,000

To show you the power of this solution, we have shared slightly modified details of a particular client's situation. Here are the assumptions:

- Husband and wife have $20,000,000 of assets in their taxable estate.
- Assets are expected to grow at 10% per year (after tax).
- Joint life expectancy is approximately twenty years.

- The couple wants to protect those funds from lawsuits and eliminate unnecessary estate tax liabilities.
- They want to retain access to these funds during their lifetime.
- They want to protect their children's inheritances from divorce, but don't want to have to risk the relationships with their children or in-laws by asking for prenuptial or postnuptial agreements.

We calculated the impact planning could offer them. We assumed the projected combined federal estate tax and state inheritance taxes would be 55%. You could look at this estimate as the highest federal estate rate in the last twenty years. Alternatively, you could support this estimate with today's low 40% estate tax rate and a 15% state inheritance tax rate (the highest in any state is now 18%). Of course, it is uncertain when the clients will die, and we can't know what the combined tax rate will be at that time.

After meeting with the lawyers and with our team to discuss the plan and the potential benefits (which you will see shortly), the clients decided to move forward with the SLAT transaction. The process took fewer than ninety days. Here are the steps they took:

- Each spouse created a SLAT for the benefit of the other spouse and the children. The terms of the two trusts were substantially different enough to be compliant with IRS guidelines.

- The husband made a gift of $10,000,000 of separate property to the SLAT for wife, children, and future grandchildren.
- The wife made a gift of $10,000,000 of separate property to the SLAT for husband, children, and small amounts for cousins.
- The clients moved existing life insurances on each other to the proper trusts.
- The clients filed gift tax returns, utilized most of their $23 million exemption, paid $0 tax, and removed all these assets from their estate.
- Total fees for planning, legal structures, and gift tax returns were $34,000.

Potential Results at Time of Second Death

With HIS and HERS SLAT:	$134,550,000 net to heirs
Without SLAT Planning:	$60,547,500 net to heirs
Value of SLAT Planning:	$74,002,500 net to heirs

By spending a couple of months in the planning, and less than $34,000, the clients created the creditor protection they desired, protected their kids and grandkids from unnecessary taxes and the threat of divorce, and enhanced their total estate by $74,000,000.

YOUR BETTER PATH

We are not attorneys and have no financial incentive to send you to a law firm to create this SLAT structure. If you do use this technique, you will remove over $27 million and all its future growth from your taxable estate. This will save you money you might otherwise pay me to help you transfer in the future. Despite a perceived conflict of interest that I might have to recommend this strategy to you, I am begging you to seriously consider this technique. It is the easiest, quickest, most impactful solution you can use to take a huge dent out of the friction you will encounter when trying to pass wealth to the next generation.

The "his and hers" SLATs allow you to remove over $27 million from your taxable estate while still having access to those funds. The technique protects those assets from any creditors you and your spouse may have. It also protects all the growth of those assets from both estate taxes and creditors. This truly is a get-out-of-taxes free card that should save your family up to $10 million. If you only acted on one thing in this entire book, this is one of three strategies that deserves very serious consideration.

CHAPTER 21

LLCs ARE MAGICAL ESTATE PLANNING TOOLS

Do you recall the two most important goals of planning? Efficiency and flexibility. First, we want to get as much leverage out of anything we spend time or money doing. Almost everyone complains about a shortness of time or money, if not both. Second, we want to embrace the fact that change is the only constant in life. Flexibility is paramount in our planning. In Sections 2 and 3, we explained how limited liability companies (LLCs) can be used to protect assets and reduce unnecessary taxes. Here's the trifecta—LLCs are superior estate planning tools, too.

ESTATE PLANNING BENEFITS OF LLCs

There are three major benefits you can leverage for your estate planning.

LLC assets **avoid probate and continue without delays**. Even if you ignore the advice in this section and don't title your LLC interests in your living trust, the assets in your LLC do not go through probate—only your interest in the LLC will. If you structure your LLC so that your intended beneficiaries are successor managers, they will control the LLC and its assets after you die. They will have control over the LLC assets or business during the probate process. Because probate can last several years, this continued control can be crucial for operating a business or real estate interests, preventing sizable erosion of assets (as we saw with the Bronson family previously).

LLCs allow you to remove property from your taxable estate **without giving up control.** The main objection (to estate planning) is giving up control of the property while still alive. You can hold the 1% managing membership interests of any LLC and have the best of both worlds. By gifting up to 99% (non-managing) membership interest of your LLCs, you still control all the LLC assets—while subjecting only 1% of your assets to estate taxes. Let's see how this works.

CASE STUDY: TERRANCE'S INVESTMENTS

Terrance, a sixty-three-year-old proctologist, had almost $1.8 million dollars in a Schwab account. He created an LLC to own the portfolio, naming himself as the sole managing member. At the outset, he owned 2% as a managing member, 93% as a member, and gifted 1% to each of his five grandchildren. Because this 1% was worth approximately $18,000 (the annual gift tax limit), there were no gift taxes due.

Terrance can gift each grandchild $18,000 in LLC interests each year. Because Terrance is married, he and his wife Stephanie can gift $36,000 annually to each grandchild. Over the next ten years (assuming no changes in gift limits), Terrance and Stephanie can gift over $1.8 million worth of LLC interests to grandchildren—with $0 of gift taxes. Because Terrance is the managing member of the LLC, he retains control over the investments, so the grandkids can't squander the money. He and Stephanie get the best of both worlds—reduction of estate taxes without giving up control.

LLC interests may be discounted. Do you remember a time in your childhood before you had a bank account? Can you remember giving money to one of your parents "to hold for you" until you needed it? Do you remember having to ask for your money, and having them ask you, "What do you need $10 for?"

Whether your parents were easy or difficult with money, you can appreciate how there is a difference between having the money and having to ask someone else for it. Which money is worth more to you—the money you control, or the money someone else controls?

The IRS has recognized for decades that non-controlling interest of corporations, LLCs, and partnerships deserve some type of "discounts" for lack of control. They have also acknowledged that there may be additional discounts for lack of marketability—for closely held businesses or illiquid family interests. Because LLCs allow for interests that are non-managing, those interests may be worth as little as seventy or seventy-five cents on the dollar (a 25% to 30% discount).

LET'S REVISIT THE TERRANCE EXAMPLE

Let's assume Terrance and Stephanie pass away owning only 25% (non-managing) membership interests in the LLC that has a $4,000,000 value. For simplicity, let's also assume they have no other assets and they have already used up their lifetime exemptions. This example should demonstrate the powerful benefit that LLCs offer families who may be worth enough to generate estate tax liabilities.

HOW MIGHT THE LLC BE VALUED FOR ESTATE TAX PURPOSES?

Their attorneys argued that there were both marketability discounts and the minority ownership discount to consider. The lack of marketability discount exists because Terrance's five grandchildren own the other LLC interests, so nonfamily members would not be interested in buying his interests.

Under the LLC agreement, the interests are not freely transferable. The minority ownership discount may be applied because Terrance and Stephanie own only 25% of the LLC at death. Attorneys argued that a 30% discount would be appropriate.

Valuation of Limited Liability Company Interests				
Your % Ownership in LLC	X	Fair Market Value of Total LLC Assets	X	Discount Factor
25%	X	$4,000,000	X	70%

The remaining million dollars in the LLC was valued at $700,000 in the estate tax return. At a 40% estate tax rate, this simple planning saved the family over $120,000. This is in addition to the $1,200,000 (40% tax rate X $3 million of value previously gifted using annual gifts and their appreciation).

For less than $25,000 of fees for set up, reporting, and gifting, Terrance and Stephanie saved their family over $1,300,000 in unnecessary taxes and fees without ever really giving up control of the accounts.

YOUR BETTER PATH

LLCs are tremendous estate planning tools. These benefits are in addition to their significant asset protection and tax-saving benefits. It is hard to imagine how any plan could be complete without at least one or two LLCs. Between the authors, we have nearly a dozen as part of our family planning strategies. These structures provide extraordinary wealth building, strategic planning, and tax management benefits. If necessary, feel free to go back to Sections 2 and 3 to review some of these benefits.

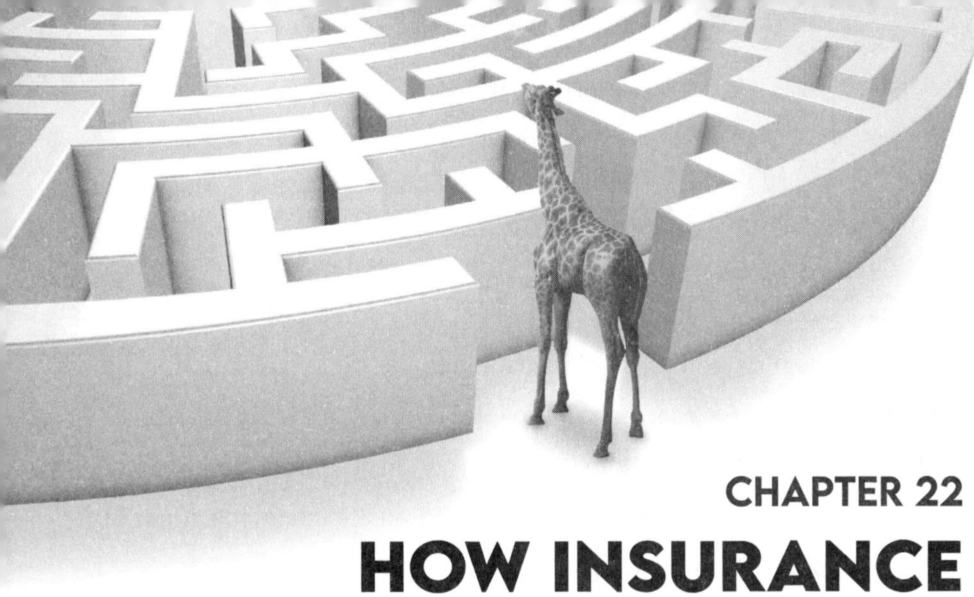

CHAPTER 22

HOW INSURANCE FITS INTO ESTATE PLANNING

In the last chapter, we explored how the LLC can supercharge your estate planning. This is in addition to the asset protection and tax-saving benefits discussed earlier. In this chapter, we will explore how permanent, or cash value, life insurance can be tailored to provide some valuable estate liquidity, help balance an estate where some children are in the business and others may not be and can be used as invaluable collateral for wealth transfers for very wealthy families. All of this is in addition to the asset protection, tax-free accumulation, and disaster avoidance benefits we covered in other sections.

WHY YOU HATE LIFE INSURANCE

If you hate life insurance, you're in good company. We have spent decades trying not to sell life insurance for fear of being lumped in with people. . .well, people who sell life insurance! OMG, that might be worse than being called a lawyer! All kidding aside, we have seen countless insurance policies—premiums, cash values, and death benefits—wasted unnecessarily. If you apply for life insurance the right way, look for the right type of policy for you, manage policies properly, and own them properly, you can get so much more bang for your buck. Unfortunately, there are millions of professionals who give advice on life insurance. Most of them are lucky if they understand one or two of these areas:

DISCIPLINES IMPACTING LIFE INSURANCE

Accounting	*Asset protection*
Underwriting	*Product selection*
Income taxation	*Estate planning*
Business planning	*Partnership tax*
Financial planning	*Business valuation*
Retirement planning	*Investment management*

Can you see how it's so difficult to have a strong working knowledge of all the things that go into buying, owning, and managing a policy correctly? Is it any wonder that so many people are frustrated with the insurance industry?

Let's go over a few of the biggest mistakes so you get the most out of your insurance. Then, we will show some of the more creative and powerful ways to use life insurance in your highly efficient and flexible plan.

HOW TO SAVE MONEY ON LIFE INSURANCE

How many times have you seen an advertisement to buy life insurance quickly and painlessly online for pennies? Cue the barista getting $2 million of life insurance for $3.76/month. What they fail to tell us is the type and duration of insurance, whether it has cash value, and more importantly, what quality company would give a barista $2 million in coverage unless they owned the coffee shop?!?

You should absolutely try to save money on your life insurance but not by cutting corners. When most people talk about saving on life insurance they are only thinking about their premium, and that is certainly a good place to start. But saving money on life insurance also includes the accumulation phase of a cash value life insurance policy and the distribution phase, too.

Underwriting is the first opportunity to save money on life insurance. There are over a dozen classifications based on health, and they vary widely between carriers. Moving two classes could increase your insurance costs by 75 – 100%. Managing your underwriting properly could save your family millions of dollars. The best way to determine what company will provide you with the most favorable underwriting is to perform an informal inquiry which can then be used to estimate who the best fit may be.

Did you know there are over 200 life insurance companies and 3,000 products available—not counting term insurance? Most agents will be familiar with no more than a handful of companies and maybe a dozen products. Are you sure that your agent found the best product and company for you? Be careful of anyone who is affiliated with, or does most of their business with, one company, as they are often incentivized to sell a certain amount of that company's product.

We once met a business owner who called us in to review their estate plan. We will call him Rufus. Rufus had a thriving multigenerational business and a net worth of approximately $20 million. He was concerned about how much he was paying for his life insurance on an annual basis and wanted a fresh set of eyes on things. Upon reviewing his estate "plan," we discovered that an agent affiliated with a major carrier had implemented a "strategy" requiring Rufus to buy more and more life insurance as he became more successful! Great for the agent, but it didn't solve the problem of Rufus' estate, which could have been solved cheaply with SLATs for him and his wife.

During the conversation, Chris pointed out to Rufus that he had five separate insurance products from the same carrier. He then asked Rufus what he thought the odds of that carrier having the best product in each of these five categories. Rufus' response was, "not a chance."

Product structure also plays a critical role in saving on life insurance. You are either buying a policy for income or you are buying a policy for liquidity. In the first case, you want maximum accumulation and minimum death benefit. In the second, you want minimum cash accumulation and maximum death benefit. Too many people buy policies that try to accomplish both. You may think you are saving on your insurance, but you end up getting far less (of both) than you could have secured from two separate policies.

The last place we see people make the biggest mistake when trying to save on life insurance premiums is ownership. If you own policies in your own name, they are part of your taxable estate. This could cause your family to unnecessarily lose upwards of 50% to estate taxes at death. If your policy was owned in your spouse's SLAT (and vice versa), the cash values would be available to the spouse and the death benefit proceeds would be available to the spouse and the next generation beneficiaries, completely free of estate taxes.

CREATIVE STRATEGIES FOR MAXIMIZING INSURANCE PROCEEDS

Now that we know how to save money on the front end when buying life insurance, let's look at some innovative strategies to get even more out of life insurance.

Most people would be surprised to find out that you can own a policy for your spouse inside your retirement plan, such as a 401(k). You can use pre-tax dollars to pay for a life insurance policy that will pay tax-free benefits to your beneficiaries. We helped a wealthy business owner turn $3,000,000 of retirement plan assets (which would have been taxed at 80% to his heirs—income and estate tax) into over $10 million of tax-free death benefit to the kids and grandkids. This really does work!

Convertible term life insurance provides a straightforward method to secure a significant death benefit when you're young and healthy. With the option to convert the policy to whole life or universal life later, you avoid the need to undergo new underwriting. This simple, yet effective, technique allows you to maximize the amount of coverage per dollar spent while locking in insurability at a younger age. This provides planning flexibility as your financial needs evolve.

If you have a cash value life insurance policy that is no longer needed for its original purpose (supplemental retirement income), you can convert it into a policy focused solely on providing a death benefit. This is kind of like trading in your minivan after the kids grow up and move out. You don't need all that space, so you can get something faster or more luxurious.

By using a 1035 exchange, covered in Section 3, you exchange the cash value built up in your policy to secure a new policy with significantly more death benefit. We recently helped a retired woman more than double the death benefit she will leave her children by exchanging her policy for one that better suited her needs.

Using life insurance as a corporate benefit can be a unique way to attract and retain key employees *and* create more benefits for owners at the same time. Generally, when a company offers life insurance as part of their benefits package, it is a small amount of annual renewable term insurance that disappears if you leave your employer. By offering cash value life insurance, you not only provide valuable protection for the employees but also tax-advantaged benefits to both the employer and the employee. Additionally, life insurance can be used in executive compensation packages, leveraging its tax-free benefits as a unique perk or golden handcuff. This is covered in greater detail in ***giraffeMONEY*** under the name TrEE (which means Transforming Expenses into Equity).

Every so often we come across someone who purchased a death-benefit-focused life insurance policy who no longer needs the protection or wants to pay their premiums. Before surrendering a life insurance policy for its cash value or allowing it to lapse, creating a potentially taxable event, consider selling it through a life settlement. Selling a policy may provide a higher payout than surrendering it, offering an alternative way to recoup some of the investment in premiums paid over the years.

These are just a few ways to maximize your policy benefits when used creatively in a comprehensive plan. They highlight the importance of understanding the various uses of life insurance beyond its traditional role and tailor coverage to meet your goals. In Section 5, we will learn about using life insurance to protect your business.

YOUR BETTER PATH

Life insurance is probably the most misunderstood, and most despised, component of any financial plan. This is evidenced by how many people tell us they flat out hate life insurance—on one hand; then there are dozens of very successful business owners and extraordinarily wealthy families who spend millions of dollars annually on life insurance—on the other.

The people who hate life insurance aren't wrong. The people who spend millions on annual premiums aren't stupid. Like most complicated tools and strategies, life insurance can be a huge waste of money or an invaluable piece of your plan.

How you buy, own, and use life insurance can have a profound effect on how that insurance will benefit you, your family, or your business. It is very important that you work with your team of advisors to determine how to plan, acquire, utilize, and manage insurance in your planning.

ESTATE PLANNING SUMMARY

Estate planning is often thought of as something only the rich and fabulous must do. Since the only certainties are death and taxes, everyone needs an estate plan to protect their family's time and money. Before you move into the next section, "Avoid Financial Disasters," let's review the key takeaways from this section:

1. **Estate Planning Is Essential:** Without proper planning, families will face unnecessary taxes, delays, and disputes. Letting governments and courts decide how your estate should be settled is never a good idea.
2. **You Need a Will and a Living Trust:** A will gives guidance, but the living trust has all the power. The combination of these two can keep your estate private, eliminate all probate fees, protect your heirs, and save your family millions of dollars in taxes.
3. **The Secret Weapon:** Spousal Lifetime Access Trusts (SLATs) let you have your cake and eat it too. Eliminate all taxes on $30 million estates (and all future growth) without giving up any access to the assets. Over 99% of families can simplify their estate planning with the living trust and SLATs—and be done.
4. **Use LLCs for Leverage and Flexibility:** When you are uncertain about your future, LLCs help avoid probate, maintain control over assets or a business, and facilitate tax-efficient transfers.
5. **Use Life Insurance Strategically:** This is done by combining cost-saving measures and integrating

life insurance with LLCs, SLATs, or irrevocable life insurance trusts. Whether you need estate liquidity, balanced inheritances for heirs, mechanisms for executive compensation, or collateral for very large wealth transfers, life insurance can be a surprisingly efficient and powerful tool.

6. **Save Money on Life Insurance:** Make sure you don't overpay for the appropriate coverage. Secure convertible term when you are young and healthy. Get a review of your life insurance every three to five years. Most people significantly overpay for life insurance because they don't know what their options are.
7. **Be Flexible and Proactive with Planning:** By leveraging multiple tools and strategies, you can give yourself options. Life, taxes, legislation, and the economy will all change. Your plan will need to evolve and adapt to these changes.
8. **Don't Follow the Herd:** Most Americans fail to plan, and most of the plans that are created are woefully inadequate. Understanding and avoiding common estate planning mistakes, like relying solely on joint ownership or having only a will, can prevent future pain for your heirs.

ESTATE PLANNING CHECKLIST

To avoid unnecessary expenses, delays, and aggravation, we recommend you consider:

	Gather Information
	List of assets (real estate, investments, retirement accounts, life insurance policies, etc.)
	Debts (mortgages, loans, credit card balances, etc.)
	Make a list of important documents (will, trust documents, deeds, titles, insurance policies, etc.) and mark down the dates they were done and reviewed.

	Define Your Goals
	Determine how you want your assets distributed.
	Consider who you want to manage your affairs if you become incapacitated.
	Decide on healthcare preferences and appoint someone to make medical decisions for you if you can't make them for yourself.

	Create Essential Documents:
	A Last Will and Testament specifies how your assets should be distributed after your death and appoints a guardian for minor children.
	Establish Living Trust (family trust, loving trust, A-B Trust) to avoid probate, keep your estate private, and reduce taxes.
	A Power of Attorney designates someone to make financial or medical decisions on your behalf if you become unable to do so.
	An Advance Directive outlines your healthcare preferences and appoints a healthcare proxy to make medical decisions for you if you're incapacitated.

It is very important to review and update your estate plan on a regular basis, typically every five years, and whenever there is a major life event. It is important to consult with your team of advisors to review and update goals, financial status, documents, beneficiaries, and changes to the tax regime. As always, be sure to communicate changes to your loved ones and key individuals involved with executing your wishes.

Once you have made sure that you have addressed the basics, you can then start to look towards more advanced estate-planning techniques. Many of these tools serve specific roles and may only be useful as your wealth accumulates. Familiarizing yourself with them can help you ensure you don't miss the window of opportunity to use a technique that can protect a significant portion of your family's wealth before you've outgrown it.

1. Irrevocable Life Insurance Trust (ILIT): Establishing an ILIT to hold life insurance policies outside of the taxable estate, providing liquidity to pay estate taxes and other expenses while potentially avoiding estate tax.
2. Family Limited Partnership (FLP) or Limited Liability Company (LLC): Transferring assets into a FLP or LLC to centralize management, maintain control, and potentially leverage valuation discounts for gift and estate tax purposes.
3. Grantor Retained Annuity Trust (GRAT): Transferring appreciating assets into a GRAT, which allows the grantor to receive an annuity payment for a specified

term, with any remaining assets passing to beneficiaries free of gift tax.

4. Charitable Remainder Trust (CRT) or Charitable Lead Trust (CLT): Establishing a CRT to provide income to beneficiaries for a specified period, with the remainder passing to charity, or a CLT to provide income to charity for a specified period, with the remainder passing to beneficiaries.
5. Dynasty Trust: Creating a dynasty trust to transfer assets to future generations while potentially avoiding estate tax for multiple generations.
6. Employee Stock Ownership Plan (ESOP): Utilizing an ESOP to facilitate the transfer of ownership in a closely held business to employees while potentially providing tax advantages.

Utilizing advanced estate planning strategies requires careful consideration of legal, tax, and financial implications and may involve complex structures, documentation, and legal fees. Consulting with experienced professionals, including estate planning attorneys, tax advisors, and financial planners, is crucial to implement these strategies in alignment with your desires.

SECTION 5

DON'T GET EATEN ALIVE—AVOID FINANCIAL DISASTERS

Having ambitious financial goals, and vigilantly pursuing them, are both integral to success. Unfortunately, vision and dedication are not enough to guarantee it. You must avoid catastrophic financial losses on your journey.

By this point in the book, it should be clear that YOU are your greatest asset. You have been investing in yourself throughout the first four sections of ***giraffeMONEY Essentials***. This section will teach you how to protect your family, your business, and your wealth from the two most dangerous and most damaging threats that exist:

- Dying prematurely; and
- Becoming disabled (from injury or debilitating illness).

In either case, the emotional and financial damages of either of these events can undo lots of great planning for a family or a business. Once you create safeguards against these unforeseen disasters, you can more confidently move forward building, enjoying, and sharing wealth.

CHAPTER 23
PREMATURE DEATH

The emotional distress caused by the premature death of a loved one cannot be exaggerated; however, long before the psychological scars begin to heal, financial devastation may begin for surviving family members. Consider these statistics: 460,000 people suffered strokes in 2019, and 150,005 died. (American Heart Association).

- In 2019, an American had a 1 in 19 chance (5.3%) of dying from a stroke.
- Accidents accounted for 173,041 deaths in 2019 (U.S. Centers for Disease Control and Prevention).
- Accident was the No. 3 leading cause of death in the U.S. and the No. 1 cause of death among people aged 1 to 44 years.

Note: Accidental death is increasing in rate much more quickly than the four other leading causes of death: heart disease, cancer, stroke, and chronic lower respiratory diseases. As recently as 2006, stroke was the third-leading cause of death while accident was fifth.

INCOME PROTECTION

The obvious financial effect of death, especially for younger families, is lost income. What's the impact on the survivors? If you aren't there to provide, the family likely hasn't saved enough for living expenses, therapy for survivors, future retirement plan contributions, education costs for kids, expenses to care for aging parents or special needs siblings, or children's weddings (these are the items most often mentioned by our clients in our discussions). Most families don't save enough for these items until the income earners are well into their 50s, and many don't get there until they are in their 60s. The first step is figuring out how much life insurance your family needs to replace the income of each parent. Consider these approaches to calculating insurance needs:

- **Income replacement.** The present value of twenty years of lost income for an individual with $74,580 of AFTER-TAX INCOME (which is $100,000 to $110,000 of pre-tax income) is approximately $1,013,566. That means that, at the time of death, the family would be in the same financial situation if they had twenty years of future income or had a lump sum of $1,013,566 today (with an average annual return of 4%).

  For a breadwinner earning $350,000 per year after tax (approx. $500,000 gross income), the present value of twenty years of lost income is more than $4.76 million (with the same average annual return of 4%). This simple estimate for income replacement is that you need approximately 14 times the after-tax income, or 10 times the gross pre-tax earnings, of the breadwinner to replace twenty years of lost income. If you have a younger breadwinner who intends to work thirty more years, the multiples go up to 20 times after-tax income or 15 times the gross pre-tax earnings.

- **Lump sum.** Some families are unsure if their current earnings are enough, or are more than enough, to meet future obligations. They prefer to add up the needs: $300,000 for college x 3 kids = $900,000. Home mortgage – $600,000. $2,000,000 for my spouse to live on until the kids are older and he/she gets back to working full-time. In this case, the family would buy $900k + $600k + $2M = $3.5 million of life insurance.

It is also worth considering whether the surviving spouse will be employable at a meaningful level when the children are providing for themselves. Even if the surviving spouse had a lucrative career prior to having children, spending twenty or more years out of the workforce could completely erase the value of prior experience or advanced degrees.

ESTATE PRESERVATION

Section 4 focuses on ways to preserve a family's estate, so we won't spend too much time on it here. If a sudden death involves the loss of both a husband and a wife (or the second of the two of them dies), there could be significant estate tax liabilities and business interruption (discussed in the next chapter). As you may recall from Section 4, the second death in a family with a net worth over $5 million could result in estate taxes of approximately 50%.

Without the liquidity necessary to pay the taxes, continue paying mortgages, and find a replacement to maintain the business, a family may be forced to sell real estate or a family business. A rushed sale almost always results in a lower sale price. If the market isn't particularly good when you must sell to generate liquidity, families might see losses of value ranging from 30% to 80%.

Purchasing adequate life insurance is the fastest and most cost-effective way to mitigate this risk. Why? Because insurance requires annual or monthly premiums payments. This can be done while the family invests and starts saving a safety-net side fund—which can take a decade or two to build.

YOUR BETTER PATH

All significant earners in the family must have life insurance. Because life insurance is less expensive when the applicant is younger and healthier (and possibly unavailable if you develop serious health issues), we strongly suggest securing adequate life insurance as early as possible. This can be accomplished by securing convertible term life insurance. It is significantly less expensive than permanent life insurance and can be incrementally converted to permanent insurance as your needs change.

You learned some interesting facts about life insurance in Sections 2, 3, and 5. You know that many states offer complete protection of the cash values of life insurance policies. You know that cash values also grow tax-free inside of properly structured policies. Life insurance policies can create liquidity to pay estate taxes, to balance an estate between heirs, and as a tool for executive compensation. For those of you who own businesses and have partners, the next chapter will explain how devastating a death can be to a business, the partners, and the partners' families—and how to mitigate that risk more efficiently.

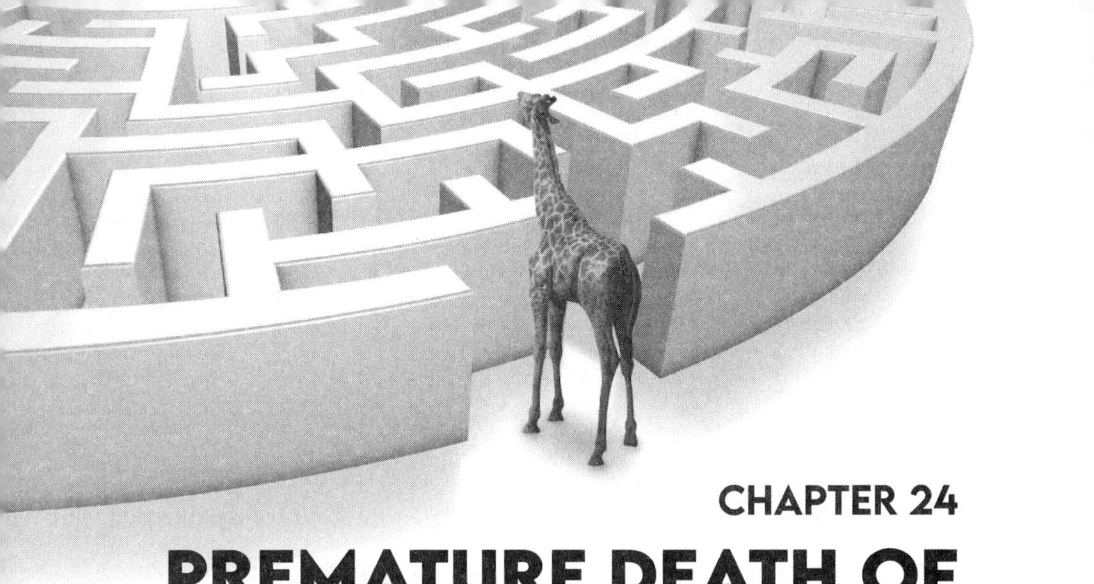

CHAPTER 24
PREMATURE DEATH OF A BUSINESS PARTNER

Though the odds of premature death in the family and business context are nearly the same (though some would argue the self-employed suffer more stress-related injuries and die earlier), we find that businesses address this risk even less frequently than families do. This is disturbing because business owners are responsible to the other owners, the employees, and to the customers. Don't let these stakeholders down by ignoring the very real possibility of a premature death.

ALWAYS EXPECT THE UNEXPECTED

Owners of a business or professional practice often spend ten to fourteen hours per day, six or seven days per week getting their businesses to the point where they can provide a measure of security for their families. We know because we are business owners ourselves. Nonetheless, those who ignore one fundamental legal contract jeopardize all their hard work. This very important legal contract is the buy-sell agreement. It is an agreement that all owners sign agreeing to how the business will be valued at the time of one partner's death or disability and how the purchase of the shares will be paid.

Without a buy-sell agreement, partners and surviving family have no legally enforceable plan for what will happen at a time when the family is grieving and possibly struggling to pay its bills. Naturally, members of that family will look to the surviving business partners for help and support in their time of need. At the same time, the surviving partners may be struggling to get by without the skillset of a valuable owner. The last thing either of these two groups need is a struggle over money. In too many cases, the absence of a buy-sell agreement at the time of death can cause bankruptcies of the owners or a forced sale of the business at fire sale values.

The buy-sell agreement is just as important for the families of the surviving partners as they need funds to buy out the deceased partner's family and continue with their business. Let's consider some of the questions that savvy business owners ask themselves:

- What will happen when a partner dies?
- Do I want my partners' spouse or children as my new partners?
- If not, could I afford to buy them out at that time?
- What happens to my share of the business if I want to exit the business or retire?
- What happens if any of my partners become disabled or get into messy divorces?
- Will I have to take on their spouses as partners? (Anyone see *Ted Lasso*?)

- What happens to my family if I die or become disabled?
- How can I ensure they get their fair share of the business?

Let's take a quick look at the case study of Fred and Ernie. Their story of a two-person firm losing one partner is unfortunately too common.

CASE STUDY: FRED AND ERNIE

Fred and Ernie are owners of a $10 million (annual revenue) printing company. Fred has the sales expertise, while Ernie runs the production side of the operation. Their overall profitability results from their joint efforts. If Fred were to die prematurely, Ernie would have to either hire a new employee or promote someone to fill Fred's position. A new hire would be expensive and unlikely to duplicate Fred's results for awhile, if ever.

At the same time, Fred's widow would want to continue to take the same money out of the business that she and Fred received before his death. If Fred's widow is raising a young family or has children in college, she may be in a financial position where she is forced to sell Fred's shares of the company. Considering few buyers would want to buy a non-controlling interest in a company, Ernie might need to sell the business at a distressed price just to meet the needs of his late partner's family.

Maybe Fred's son is also in the business and has his own ideas about how things should be run. Perhaps Fred's spouse wants to see Fred's son take over in his father's place. It wouldn't matter that little Fredo is incompetent. Without proper planning, it may be impossible for Ernie to continue a profitable business under such circumstances. Choosing between selling your company at a discount or partnering with your late partner's grieving spouse or child is no choice at all. The best tool for solving the dilemmas that arise from these questions is the buy-sell agreement in its various forms.

THE BUY-SELL AGREEMENT

A buy-sell agreement is an agreement that all owners sign that stipulates how the business will be valued at the time of one partner's death or disability and how the purchase of the deceased partner's shares will be paid. Buy-sells can be used for corporations, partnerships, limited partnerships, limited liability companies (LLCs), and other business structures.

BENEFITS TO THE BUSINESS AND ITS OWNERS

A properly planned buy-sell agreement will provide for the orderly continuation of the ownership and control of the business. By providing a means for valuation, and a method of paying out the purchase of one partner's shares, the buy-sell prevents unnecessary conflict. There is no need for tense negotiations with grieving survivors, nor any chance of unwanted outsiders becoming owners.

BENEFITS TO FAMILY MEMBERS

For a deceased owner's family, the existence of the buy-sell can ensure the family or estate has a liquid asset rather than an illiquid minority interest in a privately held business that would be difficult to sell. The agreement may provide a valuation of the business interest, which can be used for estate tax filing purposes. This may save the survivors the additional headache and expense of securing another valuation and fighting the Internal Revenue Service on that value.

FUNDING THE AGREEMENT

Because the buy-sell agreement contemplates a buy-sell transaction at the time of an owner's death or disability, insurance policies are generally recommended to fund the transaction. There are many reasons for this, including the following:

- Insurance policies pay a predetermined amount, with proceeds available at exactly the time when they are needed as a funding source (no liquidity concerns).
- Proceeds will be available regardless of the financial state of the business that may result from the partner's death (if premiums have been paid).
- Proceeds will be available regardless of the personal financial challenges of any of the remaining partners (lawsuits, divorce, or bad investments may otherwise tie up partners' assets if insurance were not in place).
- Insurance premiums cost the business less in capital than it would to save money in a buyout fund.
- The risks of premature death and disability of owners are shifted to the insurer.
- Insurance proceeds are paid to the owner or owner's family income-tax-free.

Absent a requirement for insurance policies to fund the benefit, it is important to consider some type of security arrangement for the departing owner. These agreements might include personal guarantees from remaining owners, mortgages or security interests in real estate, a bank standby letter of credit, or even collaterally assigned life insurance policies.

YOUR BETTER PATH

As with any planning, the early bird is richly rewarded. Nowhere in business planning is this truer than in buy-sell agreements. The reason for this is not so much economic as political. If this planning is done before an owner is close to disability, divorce, retirement, or death, all owners are in similar positions, making the negotiation of a standard deal for all owners much easier. Planning early for a buy-sell agreement will truly benefit you, your family, your business partners, and your business. To avoid financial disaster, consider this agreement as an essential part of your financial planning.

Buy-sell agreements don't only protect against death. They also protect against disability, which can also devastate a family. Disability income insurance is discussed later in this section. In the next chapter, we will touch on the added leverage and flexibility of life insurance.

CHAPTER 25

LIFE INSURANCE BASICS

Life insurance has been mentioned in multiple sections of this book. We would be remiss in not explaining the different types of policies. At the most basic level, life insurance pays out a benefit when someone dies. In more complicated scenarios, life insurance is the funding vehicle for millions of dollars of compensation for CEOs and your favorite Big Ten and SEC football coaches and as collateral for hundreds of millions of dollars of family wealth transfers. Yes, we have knowledge of exactly how these have been built.

Before we can build a house, we must pour a foundation. This chapter will help you better understand types of insurance, what makes them different, and some pros and cons of each type. We will explain how convertible term life insurance is an easy way to build flexibility into your planning. Then, we will explain the nuances of the different cash value, or permanent, life insurance policies and how they can be tailored to work for you.

We will cover whole life, universal life, variable life, equity-indexed life, and a very powerful tool of the rich and famous, private placement life insurance (PPLI).

TERM LIFE INSURANCE

"Term" provides coverage for a specific term or period, typically ranging from five to thirty years. If the insured individual passes away during the term of the policy, a death benefit is paid out to the beneficiaries.

Pros: Term life insurance is usually more affordable than permanent life insurance because it does not accumulate cash value. This is the quickest and most inexpensive way to secure coverage. You can buy "convertible term" coverage when you are young and healthy, then exchange or "convert" the term to a cash value life insurance product at the same company—often without any additional health or financial underwriting—in the future.

Cons: Term life insurance premiums increase with age because the risk of death increases as people get older. Over the age of 65, the cost of a new term insurance policy becomes very expensive, often unaffordable. Term insurance is not available beyond a certain age. Term is a terrible tool for estate planning because coverage cannot be guaranteed, and rates continue to increase, making planning difficult.

CASH VALUE LIFE INSURANCE

Cash value life insurance or permanent life insurance is a category of life insurance that comes in a variety of product types. The core components of cash value life insurance are the death benefit and the cash value account. When a cash value life insurance product is initially purchased, some of the premium goes towards paying the cost of insurance and policy administration fees, while the remainder is deposited in the cash value account. Depending on the type of policy, the cash value account will be invested differently. The cash value account provides a vehicle for tax-deferred growth and loans may be taken from it free of taxes provided the policy stays in force for the remainder of your life. Because it has the cash accumulation component, CVLI can play a role in tax reduction, wealth accumulation, asset protection, estate planning, and executive compensation.

WHOLE LIFE INSURANCE (WL)

Whole life insurance provides coverage for the entire lifetime of the insured individual if premiums are paid. It includes a death benefit as well as a cash value component that accumulates over time, offering a guaranteed rate of return. Premiums are usually fixed and higher compared to term life insurance.

Pros: Whole life insurance has a savings element (cash value), which is tax-deferred. The crediting rate is referred to as dividend. These typically have minimum guarantees that are much higher than the other guaranteed rates of other cash value policies.

Cons: Whole life insurance does not allow you to invest in separate accounts (e.g., money markets, stocks, and bond funds). Thus, your policy's returns will be tied to the insurance company's ability to invest its capital. It does not allow you premium flexibility or face amount flexibility.

UNIVERSAL LIFE INSURANCE

Universal life insurance is a flexible permanent life insurance policy that allows policyholders to adjust the premium and death benefit amounts within certain limits. It consists of a cash value component that earns interest over time, and policyholders can use the cash value to pay premiums or make withdrawals; however, the interest rates are not guaranteed and may fluctuate.

Pros: The product is like WL yet has more flexible premiums. It may be attractive to younger buyers who may have fluctuations in their ability to pay premiums. Because it is so flexible, universal life insurance can play many roles.

Cons: Account values are invested in the general account of the insurance company, without the same guaranteed minimum.

VARIABLE UNIVERSAL LIFE INSURANCE (VUL)

VUL is a combination of universal life insurance and variable life insurance. It offers the flexibility of universal life insurance in terms of premium and death benefit adjustments, as well as the investment component of variable life insurance.

Pros: Policyholders can allocate their premiums among different investment options, and the cash value and death benefit vary based on the performance of the selected investments. It also affords the insured another opportunity to invest in the equities markets on a tax-deferred basis.

Cons: It requires the policyholder to devote time in managing the policy's accounts. The policy's success is dependent on the investments you make. Fees are typically higher than universal life.

EQUITY-INDEXED UNIVERSAL LIFE INSURANCE (EIUL)

Equity indexed universal life insurance (EIUL) is a type of permanent life insurance policy that combines elements of both universal life insurance and indexed investment options. It offers a death benefit like other types of life insurance policies, but it also accumulates cash value over time.

Pros: Equity-indexed universal life insurance enables you to make withdrawals or borrow from the policy during your lifetime and it offers the investor the upside of the market (with a cap). Unlike variable life and variable universal life, EIUL offers the investor downside protection so the cash value will not see a negative crediting rate—even in a bad market.

Cons: Equity-indexed universal life insurance policies vary from carrier to carrier. Policies are very complicated. Cap and participation rates can be changed at the discretion of the insurance company. The minimum guaranteed returns are typically very low—0% to 2%, which is lower than most insurance products.

PRIVATE PLACEMENT VARIABLE UNIVERSAL LIFE (PPVUL)

Private placement life insurance is a specialized type of life insurance policy designed for high-net-worth individuals and institutional investors seeking to optimize their tax and estate planning strategies. PPLI is structured as a variable universal life insurance policy, offering both a death benefit and a cash value component. Here are some key characteristics of PPLI:

Customization: PPLI policies are highly customizable and tailored to the specific needs and objectives of the policyholder. They can be structured to accommodate various investment options, including hedge funds, private equity, real estate, and other alternative investments typically not available in traditional life insurance policies.

Tax Efficiency: One of the primary benefits of PPLI is its tax efficiency. The policyholder's investments within the PPLI policy grow tax-deferred, meaning they are not subject to income tax if they remain within the policy. Additionally, upon the death of the insured, the death benefit paid out to the beneficiaries is generally income tax-free under current tax laws.

Asset Protection: PPLI policies can provide a level of asset protection, as the cash value and death benefit may be shielded from creditors in certain jurisdictions. This can be particularly valuable for individuals looking to safeguard their wealth from potential lawsuits or creditor claims.

Privacy: PPLI offers a high level of privacy, as the ownership of the policy is typically held within a specially structured entity such as a trust or a limited liability company. This can help preserve the confidentiality of the policyholder's financial affairs and estate planning strategies.

It's important to note that PPLI policies are complex financial instruments that require careful consideration and expertise in tax, legal, and estate planning matters. Due diligence and consultation with qualified professionals (such as financial advisors, tax advisors, and estate planning attorneys) are essential when exploring PPLI as part of a comprehensive wealth management strategy.

Pros: Private placement variable universal life allows the client to choose hedge funds or suggest their own independent financial advisor to manage the funds within the insurance contract. Commissions tend to be much lower than traditional insurance policies. Because it combines the flexibility of variable universal life with lower fees, more investment flexibility, and investment gains within the subaccounts are not taxed, PPVUL is the ideal tool for tax reduction and retirement wealth accumulation over a long-time horizon for clients who are in high marginal tax brackets. It also affords another opportunity to invest in the equities markets on a tax-deferred basis.

Cons: Very high minimum premium requirements. Limited to accredited investors only. Because this is a private placement, there is very little written marketing material to review. Very few insurance companies do enough of this type of work to be considered efficient. Most insurance agents do not or will not sell it. The policy owner bears all the risk of the investments within the investment subaccounts.

YOUR BETTER PATH

There are many different types of life insurance policies. All of them have their place in a sound financial plan. What is important to realize is that all cash value life insurance policies offer wealth accumulation benefits and tax-free death benefits.

What you use those policies for is perhaps one of the most important questions your advisory team should answer for you. These flexible tools could be used for tax-efficient accumulation for your family, as part of an executive compensation plan, or to balance your estate among your heirs.

CHAPTER 26

LIFE INSURANCE LEVERAGE & FLEXIBILITY

In this section, we have been focusing on life insurance as a tool to help a family or business protect itself against the financial damage of an untimely death. These benefits are like those we discussed in Section 4. The main difference is that we are planning on transferring family wealth at death in the previous section, and we are protecting against unanticipated deaths in this one.

To facilitate more effective protection of widows and orphans, the tax code offers life insurance multiple tax benefits. Section 3 taught us that life insurance grows tax-deferred and can be accessed tax-free through withdrawals and policy loans. As a precursor to Section 6: Invest Wisely, it makes sense that we explore how very wealthy families and savvy business owners leverage these tax benefits, and the creditor protection mentioned in Section 2, to build tax-efficient, creditor-proof war chests within life insurance policies. Let's review some of this flexibility.

PART 1: DEATH BENEFIT

By paying relatively small amounts to an insurance company, you can protect your family. Let's consider Rob, a hard-working thirty-five-year-old who has just started a family.

Rob and his wife Ronelle have two young children, Nigel and Dikembe. Rob holds two jobs to help his family get ahead. He works in finance during the week and moonlights as a professional dancer for extra income. Ronelle is a singer. Rob knows that his family relies on his income and that the music would stop altogether if he died. With the $1,000 per month he was saving from his dancing, we were able to secure a $1.6 million life insurance policy on Rob. This policy is enough to cover his mortgage, his children's college funds, and leave Ronelle with enough money to raise the children. Now that Rob has insurance, the beat can go on for his family even if it doesn't for him.

PART 2: ESTATE PLANNING

Let's assume that Rob wins $1 million on the reality show *America's Got Talent* or Ronelle's singing career finally hits the big time, and they are making more money than they need to support their lifestyle. What do they do then?

One of the techniques they chose to implement is the creation of an irrevocable life insurance trust (ILIT). Under the ILIT, Rob and Ronelle will make $24,000 annual gifts to the trust. The trust uses the $24,000 to purchase a second-to-die life insurance policy on Rob and Ronelle. When they finally pass away, their children will receive $10 million tax-free.

PART 3: TAX-FREE ACCUMULATION AND DISTRIBUTION

Most people don't think of life insurance policies as investments; however, our very wealthy clients have used these tax-efficient investment tools for years.

Let's look at a healthy 35-year-old male, like Rob in the earlier example.

He may look at his cash value life insurance policy as his unlimited after-tax pension. The big differences between the insurance policy cash values and his pension are that he can take all (or none) of the money from the insurance policy before he reaches age 59½ without penalty. With life insurance, you don't have to contribute for employees, and the insurance policy gives you death benefit protection.

The economics of investing into a life insurance policy may look like this:

- Beginning at age 35, Rob invests $1,000 per month for 30 years.
- The policy grows at an average of 8% per year (before expenses and fees).
- Cash values in year 30, when Rob retires, are approximately $1.1 million.
- He takes tax-free policy withdrawals and policy loans of $100,000 every year from age 66 until age 90. That is $360,000 yielding more than $2.5 million of tax free retirement income.
- This amounts to between $5 and $10 million of death benefit for his family.

By leveraging the tax-free accumulation and death benefit features of cash value life insurance, Rob can protect his family from his premature death and provide a very tax-efficient investment return for himself at the same time. He can solve two planning challenges with one investment. This is what makes insurance a highly efficient investment.

YOUR BETTER PATH

Life insurance offers more leverage than any other financial tool—even the LLC. A relatively small premium payment can protect a family from a premature death, protect a business in a buy-sell arrangement, or efficiently transfer the wealth from one generation to another.

The most important characteristic of life insurance is that it is flexible. You don't have to decide exactly what you want to use the life insurance for before you buy it. You can add more premium later, gift the policy to a person or entity, sell the policy, save it for the death benefit, use the cash values for lifetime needs, return the money you took out, or not return the money you took out. The biggest misunderstanding about life insurance is that most people don't see it as an investment tool.

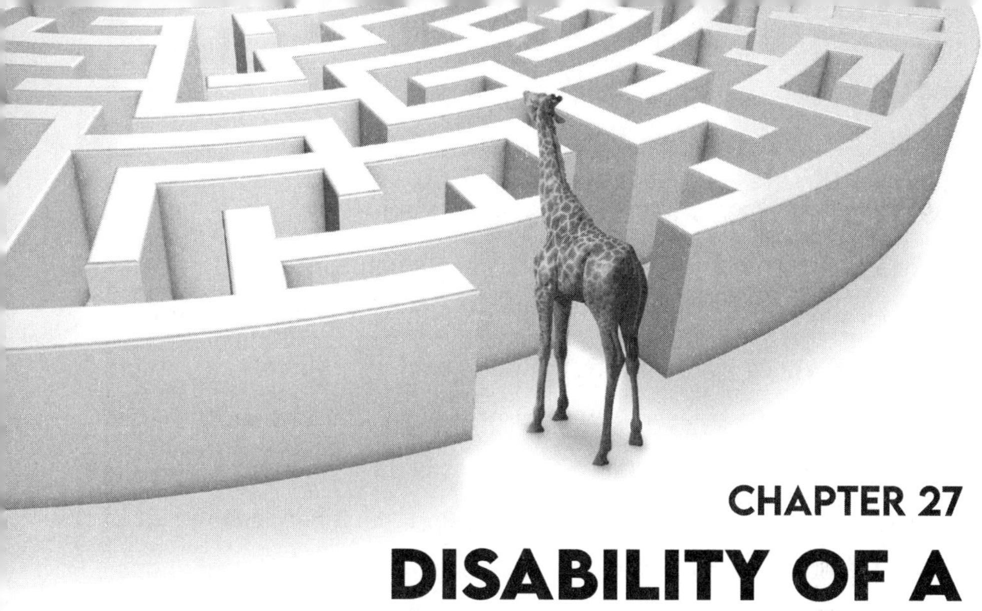

CHAPTER 27

DISABILITY OF A BREADWINNER OR BUSINESS PARTNER

NO ONE IS USELESS IN THIS WORLD WHO LIGHTENS THE BURDEN OF IT TO ANYONE ELSE.

—CHARLES DICKENS

If you are like most of our clients, the single greatest asset your family has is your earning power. This reality motivates most people to buy life insurance as protection against a premature death. Though most people we meet are underinsured, many have at least some life insurance. However, most professionals, entrepreneurs, business owners, and executives often overlook a more dangerous threat to their long-term financial stability—their own disability. This chapter explains not only why you need disability insurance, but also what to look for in a disability insurance policy.

PROTECTING INCOME FROM DISABILITY

No one ever plans on becoming disabled—though almost half of those aged 25 older or will have a disability of three months or longer at least once in their lives. In fact, the odds hold with one of the authors of this book. Chris missed 120 days of work in 1995 when he injured his back playing basketball, and another sixty days when he injured his Achilles tendon in 2014. It happened to one of us. It happens to half of the population. The odds are it will happen to either you or your spouse . . . or your business partner.

THE NEED FOR DISABILITY INSURANCE

In our opinion, disability of the family breadwinner can be more financially devastating to a family than a premature death. In both cases, the breadwinner will be unable to provide any income for the family. However, in the case of death, the deceased earner is no longer an expense to the family and may, through life insurance, leave a liquid asset behind at the time of death. If the breadwinner suddenly becomes disabled, that individual still needs to be fed, clothed, and cared for by medical professionals or family members. In many cases, medical care alone can cost hundreds of dollars per day. With a disability, income is reduced or eliminated, and expenses increase, often dramatically. This can be a devastating turn of events and can lead to creditor problems and even bankruptcy.

EMPLOYER-PROVIDED COVERAGE IS OFTEN INADEQUATE

If you are an employee, your employer may provide short-term disability insurance (STDI) and potentially long-term disability insurance (LTDI) coverage. According to a Congressional Research Service report, as of

March 2021, 42% of private industry workers had access to STDI. The length of STDI may be as low as twelve weeks and at most fifty-two weeks. For any major event, this level of coverage is a stop gap, not a solution.

In the case of LTDI, employers may limit the term of the coverage to only a few years, or the amount of benefits may only represent a small part of your compensation. Because this is most commonly an employer-paid benefit, the money received during your disability will be income taxable. For most, this results in the disabled party taking home less than half of the original amount in their paycheck after taxes are paid.

GIVE YOURSELF A CHECK-UP

Most people with employer-provided disability insurance coverage will find the benefit severely lacking. To help you determine where your coverage may be lacking, we offer a list of questions you should ask about your coverage:

- How long does the disability coverage last?
- How much is the benefit? (Different plans may cap the benefits at a certain figure, for example, $5,000 per month.)
- What percentage of your income is covered? (Generally, you cannot receive more than 60% of your income, and the benefit is capped at $7,500 or $10,000 monthly, depending on your age).
- Who pays the premiums? (Tip: If you pay the premiums yourself, and not as a deductible expense, your benefits should be tax-free.)

- Is the policy portable, or convertible, to an individual policy if you leave the company?
- If your business distributes all earnings from the corporation at year-end in the way of bonuses to all owners/partners (typical of C corporations), you should find out whether these amounts are covered by the group policy. If not, and if bonuses or commissions make up a substantial part of your income (which is the case with many people), you'll probably need supplemental coverage.
- What is the definition of disability in the group policy? Own-occupation, modified own-occupation, any occupation, or income-replacement?
- If you own the company, are your business overhead expenses covered if you are disabled? If you can't perform your duties at work, will the business keep paying you? If you can't generate income for the business, many of your expenses will keep on piling up. For professionals, a business overhead expense policy also covers hiring an outside professional to replace the insured during disability for up to two years.

GETTING THE BEST INSURANCE COVERAGE FOR THE MONEY

Now that you have given yourself a checkup and realize that you may need a new or supplemental insurance policy, you need to know what to look for to get the best coverage available at a reasonable price. The following questions are important for you to ask when considering a disability policy.

What benefit amount do you need to cover your living expenses? There are additional monthly benefits of $5,000 to $25,000 available through more specialized channels for those high earners who want more monthly income than the traditional limits.

What is the waiting period? The waiting period is the time that you must be disabled before the insurance company will pay you disability benefits. The longer the waiting period before benefits kick in, the less your premium will be. Although waiting periods can last as long as 730 days, a 180-day waiting period may give you the best coverage for your money.

How long will coverage last? It's a good idea to get a benefit period of coverage that lasts until age 65, at which point Social Security payments will begin. Be aware that many policies cover you for only two to five years.

What is the definition of disability in your policy? There are different definitions of disability within different policies at the same company and from insurance company to insurance company. The definition of disability is of the utmost importance. The main categories are own-occupation, any-occupation, and loss of income. The own-occupation policies, which pay a benefit if you can't continue your own specific occupation (even if you can and do work another occupation after the disability), are the most comprehensive, and of course, the most expensive. Two important questions you must have answered for any own-occupation policy are:

1. Are you forced to go back to work in another occupation, which may not pay as well as your current occupation?
2. Will you receive a partial benefit if you go back to work slowly after the disability and make less than you did before the disability?

Does your policy offer partial benefits? If you can work only part-time instead of your previous full-time hours, will you receive benefits? Unless your policy states that you are entitled to partial benefits, you won't receive anything unless you are completely unable to work. Also, are extended partial benefits paid if you go back to work and suffer a reduction in income because you cannot keep up the same rigorous schedule you did before you were disabled?

Important note: Partial benefits may be added on as a rider in some policies and should be seriously considered as only 3% of all disabilities are total disabilities.

Are business overhead expenses covered? When you go into business on your own, the last thing you think about is not being able to pay your bills. Whether you have $10,000 or $20,000 of monthly disability benefit, you likely don't have enough to cover your lost income and the costs of running your business.

Is your policy non-cancellable or guaranteed renewable? If a policy is non-cancellable, you will pay a fixed premium throughout the contract term. Your premium will not go up for the term of the contract. If it is guaranteed renewable, it means you cannot be canceled, but your premiums could go up.

Other issues to consider when determining if you are getting the best disability insurance coverage for your money so that you can avoid financial disasters caused by the disability of the breadwinner in your family include:

- Increased coverage
- Cost-of-living increases
- Waiver-of-premium
- Return-of-premium waiver
- Unisex pricing
- HIV rider
- Multilife pricing discounts
- Protection of future pension contributions

DISABILITY OF A BUSINESS PARTNER

The disability of a business partner can be just as financially crippling as the disability of the family breadwinner. There is a strong financial tie between business partners. There can be an even stronger financial dependency between business partners than there is between spouses. When a partner becomes disabled, the business will undoubtedly lose significant revenue while possibly facing increased costs as they attempt to fill the role of the disabled partner. Absent a buy-sell agreement tied to disability income insurance with a lump-sum payout to generate funds to buy out the disabled partner, the result could be financial devastation for the remaining partner and the business.

Even if the coverage and appropriate plan is in place to buy out the disabled partner, the remaining partner(s) are left with the financial burden of lost revenue, decreased productivity, and the cost to find and replace the disabled partner. In the event the partner isn't bought out and plans to return to the business at some point in the future, all these issues remain, and a temporary replacement may be needed.

Enter business overhead expense insurance (BOEI). The purpose of BOEI is to provide for the hardships endured by a business in the event an owner or key member of the team is disabled. Generally, BOEI covers items that are tax-deductible to the business including:

- Wages, Payroll Taxes, Benefit Contributions
- Salary for a Substitute Employee
- Debt Service
- Mortgages, Rents, and Leases
- Office Expenses
- Dues and Fees for licensing and professional organizations
- Insurance Premiums

One item of note is that BOEI does not cover the salary of the disabled owner or key employee. So even with BOEI in place an individual disability policy is necessary. It is also worth mentioning that BOEI can have a residual disability benefit for those partially disabled and a recovery benefit to assist with the owner's recovery and rehabilitation expenses.

THE BUY-SELL AGREEMENT PLUS DISABILITY POLICIES

Savvy business owners always have signed buy-sell agreements that guard against financial ruin in the event of the unexpected death or disability of a business partner. More importantly, they supplement the life insurance funding of the buy-sell agreement with lump-sum disability buyout policies on the partners to ensure that they can buy each other out in the event of either a premature death or a career-ending disability. Without the proper disability policies as part of a buy-sell agreement, a business may fail as soon as one partner becomes disabled and can no longer work.

YOUR BETTER PATH

The likelihood of a disability is greater than the probabilities of a premature death, a lawsuit, and a bankruptcy combined. Savvy business owners know that disability insurance is the only way to protect future income. We cannot overstate the importance of having a comprehensive disability policy as part of any personal financial plan and a policy as a funding mechanism for a buy-sell agreement in the case of the disability of a business partner or key employee.

INSURANCE SUMMARY

Insurance can offer both valuable protection and invaluable flexibility in your planning. Before you explore how to Invest Wisely, let's review some key takeaways:

- **Invest in Yourself:** YOU are your greatest asset; prioritize protecting yourself!
- **Protect against the Unknown:** Death and disability are the most significant risks to your financial plans. The best laid financial plans can come

crashing down if they aren't supported by the strength of the insurance cornerstone.

- **Life Insurance Is Flexible:** It can protect against disaster through multiple different types of policies. When used to accumulate cash value, insurance can be used in retirement, wealth transfer, and multiple business applications.
- **Buy-Sell Agreements Are Invaluable:** Unforeseen death or disability of a business owner can leave the surviving family members and the business in a shambles. This is the single most important agreement for any business. It provides a framework and a plan for facilitating the smooth transition of ownership.
- **Disability Insurance Is Overlooked but Essential:** Half of adults will suffer a disability during prime earning years. Corporate coverage is often severely inadequate. Look into individual coverage before it's too late.
- **Protect Your Business with Overhead Expense Insurance:** How would your business survive without key owners? BOEI provides money for essential expenses, and even a replacement, if you can't work.

INSURANCE PLANNING CHECKLISTS

Life Insurance Planning Checklist	
	Consult a professional, a financial advisor, or insurance agent to help you navigate the complexities of life insurance.
	Determine the amount of coverage needed to protect your dependents and partners, and to cover financial obligations.
	Decide between term, whole, universal, or private placement life.
	Obtain informal underwriting to determine which carrier will provide you with the most favorable terms.
	Obtain quotes from multiple insurance providers to find the best coverage at the most competitive rates.
	Periodically review your life insurance coverage to adjust for life changes such as marriage, birth of children, or career advancements.

Disability Insurance Checklist	
	Consult a professional, a financial advisor, or insurance agent, to help you navigate the complexities of life insurance
	Determine the amount of income replacement needed to cover living expenses and financial obligations in the event of a disability.
	Evaluate group coverage through employer or associations.
	Assess the need for supplemental coverage to fill gaps in employer-provided disability insurance such as limits and portability.
	Understand any exclusions or limitations in the policy regarding pre-existing conditions or specific types of disabilities.
	Periodically review your insurance coverage.

SECTION 6

INVEST WISELY

SIMPLE AIN'T EASY.

—THELONIOUS MONK

The simplicity of wise investing may appear to be a paradox. Simple can mean easy to understand, easy to get done, or uncomplicated. Wise means having experience, knowledge, and good judgment. The purpose of this section is to share our experience and knowledge so that you can easily make good decisions and uncomplicate your life.

> Investment goals should be simple—grow your wealth without losing it.

In this section, we will help you understand the landscape of investing, point out common mistakes, and show you ways to avoid overpaying (on the front or back end) firms and advisors.

More specifically, we will explain the limitations of relying on the Nobel Prize-winning investment theory that almost every investment firm follows. You will learn the real costs of taxes, inflation, and fees that decimate returns from simple mutual funds to more complex hedge funds and private equity.

Armed with the knowledge of asset protection, taxes, estate planning, and insurance, you will be able to craft ownership structures and strategies that will facilitate the wealth-building strategies that will arise from this section.

CHAPTER 28

A NOBEL PRIZE IS NOT ENOUGH

Many investment advisors may boast that their strategy is based on a Nobel Prize-winning theory. Though this sounds impressive, it has two faults:

1. Nearly everyone's strategy is based on that same theory.
2. The theory has limitations that were acknowledged by the Nobel laureates.

Let's review the investment theory, its limitations, and ways to make it work for you.

THE MODERN PORTFOLIO THEORY AND THE CAPITAL ASSET PRICING MODEL

In 1990, the Nobel Prize in Economics was awarded to Harry Markowitz, Merton Miller, and William Sharpe for their contributions to Modern

Portfolio Theory (MPT) and the Capital Asset Pricing Model (CAPM). With apologies to Markowitz, Miller, and Sharpe, we would like to offer simplistic summaries of the CAPM and MPT. There are three concepts you must be able to grasp before putting them together to form the CAPM and MPT:

1. Types of risk
2. Risk vs. reward
3. Diversification of investments

TYPES OF RISK

The Capital Asset Pricing Model divides the risk of any investment into two types: specific (nonsystematic) risk and market (or systematic) risk. Specific risk is unique to an individual investment, while systematic risk affects all investments in the market.

RISK VS. REWARD

Over an extended period, rewards are statistically higher for those who take more risk. Individuals who forego the stability of a salary and benefits to start their own businesses may make considerably more money than those individuals who took the less risky route and went to work for someone else. Doctors and lawyers bypass the opportunity to make money right out of college. Instead, they spend more time and money going to medical school or law school and delay their income-producing careers by another three to seven years. For this risk of time and money, they are generally rewarded with higher income opportunities than other college graduates. Usually, an increased investment in time and money (risk) leads to greater income potential (reward).

DIVERSIFICATION OF INVESTMENTS

Diversification is a fancy business school term for not putting all your eggs in one basket. When applied to investments, it has two meanings. First, it means diversifying among asset classes. This is more popularly known as asset allocation, which means investing in a combination of stocks, bonds, real estate, cash, and other investment classes. Diversification also applies to the individual investments made within each asset class—not investing in a few stocks, a couple bonds, and one or two parcels of real estate.

One interesting finding of the CAPM and MPT is that within a well-diversified portfolio, specific risks cancel each other out. Basically, good luck and bad luck are showing up unexpectedly at companies every day. If you invest in enough companies, the good and bad luck impacting individual holdings in your portfolio will all cancel out. As simple as this may seem, the complicated mathematical proof and subsequent model for creating an efficient set of portfolios were worthy of a Nobel Prize.

HOW DO THE CAPM AND MPT WORK?

Once investors determine how much risk they are willing to tolerate (risk tolerance), a mathematical model constructs a portfolio that will optimize the risk-reward balance. In theory, investors maximize expected returns for any level of risk. All such maximized portfolios exist on what the geeky financial people call the "efficient frontier"—where nobody boldly went prior to 1990.

If we stick with the *Star Trek* metaphors, we will channel our inner Spock and say the hoopla around the efficient frontier is "illogical." Why? The Nobel laureates acknowledged that the CAPM and MPT are designed to work in a simplified world where:

- There are no taxes or transaction costs (see Section 3)
- All investors have identical investment horizons (Gen Z and Boomers want the same)
- All investors have identical perceptions regarding the expected returns, volatilities, and correlations of available risky investments (We all agree on something?)
- Wall Street has statues of a bull, a bear, a unicorn, and a yeti

PROBLEM NO. 1: ALL INVESTORS PAY DIFFERENT TAXES AND TRANSACTION COSTS

Tax rates vary widely. Some individuals will pay 10% on gains, while others will pay over 50%. If all your stock investments are in a Roth IRA, you will never have to worry about taxes on gains. You know from Section 3 that any investment made without consideration for taxes is unwise. . .if not foolish.

It's very common to have retirement accounts and taxable investment accounts. If you are in your prime earning years and pay 35% – 50% tax rates on marginal income, you may want to:

1. Hold interest-bearing and dividend-producing assets within a tax-favored account to avoid unnecessary taxes. This could be a Roth IRA, retirement plan, or an LLC where you are "sharing" income with a person or entity in a lower tax bracket.
2. Hold long-term growth assets in your taxable accounts. If you don't intend to sell these assets for at least one year, you will only pay 15% to 23.8% capital gains taxes when you sell. If you hold these assets in a retirement plan, you would be taxed at 35% – 50% rates on future distributions. Relying on CAPM/MPT and ignoring taxes could really hurt.

PROBLEM NO. 2: ALL INVESTORS DO NOT HAVE IDENTICAL INVESTMENT HORIZONS

Investors may need money in a month, a year, a decade, or a century. Whether you are investing for your next mortgage payment or for your grandchildren's college tuition makes a world of difference. Generally, the longer you can wait, the greater your options, the more risk you can take, and the higher you can expect your returns to be over time.

PROBLEM NO. 3: INVESTORS HAVE DIFFERENT PERCEPTIONS OF RISK AND RETURNS

Yes, the internet has seemingly made all information available to everyone. Somehow, the wealthiest 1% captured 54% of new global wealth over the past decade, and 63% of new global wealth over the last two years. Obviously, information about expected returns and volatility of investments are not equally distributed.

As far as investment availability is concerned, there is also a very wide gap. If you are only investing $100,000, you may be restricted to investments that can have very high transaction costs and taxes. If you have more than $5,000,000 to invest, you have access to unique products and your transaction costs may be considerably lower relative to the smaller investor.

Perhaps you are a fan of the show *Shark Tank*. The idea of investing in the next big thing is quite popular, as the show reaches over 10 million viewers weekly. Until recently, only accredited investors with millions of dollars could legally invest in startups. With new crowdfunding laws, everyday people can access startups. Of course, selecting companies from the hundreds of thousands launching annually is a daunting task. This year, both authors invested in Fundify.com—the only SEC approved platform that identifies and invests in startup companies on your behalf. The best part is that their monthly minimum investment is only $1. We love that startup investing, once reserved only for the largest, most powerful venture funds, is now available to everyone.

YOUR BETTER PATH

The Capital Asset Pricing Model and Modern Portfolio Theory have contributed greatly to the field of portfolio selection. These theories are the basis for the strategies used by a significant percentage of institutional investors and fund managers; however, there are huge holes in their models that require a wider breadth of knowledge for investors to maximize gains and minimize risks.

Because nearly every investment advisor uses the same strategy, you should be curious (if not skeptical) about paying fees for someone to solely build you a portfolio that looks a lot like every other portfolio. In the next chapter, we will explore the impact that fees, taxes, and inflation have on investments. Then, we have an entire chapter devoted to the differences between off-the-shelf mutual funds, lower-cost exchange-traded funds (ETFs), and more customizable accounts that are individually managed.

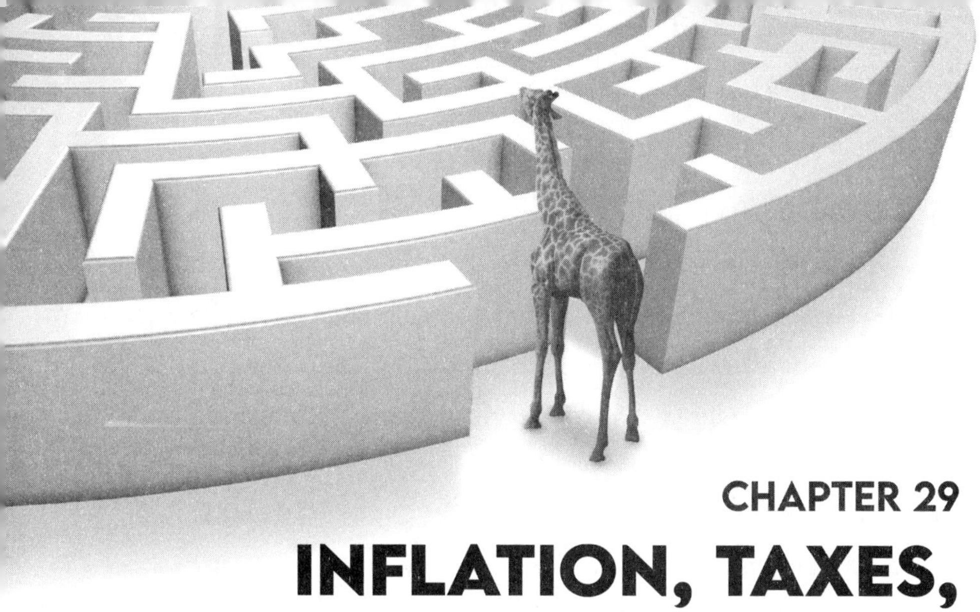

CHAPTER 29

INFLATION, TAXES, AND INVESTING

THE WAY TO CRUSH THE BOURGEOISIE IS TO GRIND THEM BETWEEN THE MILLSTONES OF TAXATION AND INFLATION.
—VLADIMIR LENIN

INFLATION IS AS VIOLENT AS A MUGGER,
AS FRIGHTENING AS AN ARMED ROBBER,
AND AS DEADLY AS A HIT MAN.
—RONALD REAGAN

INFLATION IS TAXATION WITHOUT REPRESENTATION.
—MILTON FRIEDMAN

INFLATION IS WHEN YOU PAY FIFTEEN DOLLARS FOR THE TEN-DOLLAR HAIRCUT YOU USED TO GET FOR FIVE DOLLARS WHEN YOU HAD HAIR.
—SAM EWING

The purpose of these quotes is to scare you, anger you, and then humor you—so you can smile as you add a new variable to your planning equation. It should be abundantly clear from the last four sections that **wealth is not about how much you make, it's about how much you get to keep.** Let's explore a new threat, and revisit an old one, in this chapter.

INFLATION: WHEN A DOLLAR IS WORTH ONLY 50 CENTS

You would always rather have a dollar today than a dollar tomorrow, right? There is an area of finance and economics that deals with this simple concept. They call it the time value of money. It allows us to compare the value of a dollar today to the value of a dollar in the future. When determining the present value of future dollars, many people want to know what a dollar in the future will buy them. For example, what is it worth in today's dollars? What they are really talking about is inflation.

Obviously, things become more expensive as we get older. We have all heard our parents talk about a Coke costing a nickel or a movie costing a quarter. The fact that a ticket costs $20 today is because of inflation (though many might call it highway robbery given the quality of some of today's movies). The average annual inflation rate over the past seventy years has been approximately 3.1%. This means that approximately every 22 years, things cost twice as much. During inflationary times, goods and services may double in price every four to ten years.

CALCULATING THE EFFECTS OF INFLATION

The after-tax return that an investment achieves is called the nominal return. This does not take inflation into account. When you divide the nominal return of an investment over time by the rate of inflation over that same period, you get the real rate of return, or the inflation-adjusted rate of return. Why is this important?

Let's consider why we invest. We invest because we have money we may not "need" today. We invest it, instead of spending it, because we know we will need to purchase things tomorrow.

What is our goal in investing? Beyond saving, our goal is to create greater purchasing power with our money. For example, we may invest $10,000 today with a reasonable expectation that it will be worth $20,000 in ten years. Our hope is that our $20,000 in ten years will buy more than our $10,000 would have bought us today. If we thought that inflation would exceed our investment returns, we would buy the goods now instead of investing.

Double Trouble: In 2022, the Dow Jones Average was down 8.9%, the S&P 500 Index was down 19.4%, and the Nasdaq was down 33.1%. At the same time, inflation was up 8%. This means that someone who invested in a Dow Jones fund lost 16.9% of their purchasing power. An S&P investor lost over 27% of "real" money.

Inflation in 2021 was 4.7%. In 2022, inflation was 8%. If you had money in bank accounts, money markets, CDs, or bonds during that time, you may have thought you made a little bit of money. The truth is, you lost money because the cost of goods increased at a faster rate than your investments grew. The net purchasing power of your money went down. That is inflation.

INFLATION: WHAT GOES UP MUST COME DOWN. . .RIGHT?

Inflation is when the price of goods and services goes up. Deflation is when the price of goods and services goes down. Disinflation is when the rate at which inflation is occurring slows. Stagflation has nothing to do with hunting season. It is when the rate of inflation remains elevated with high unemployment and stagnant or stilled demand for goods and services in a country.

Though harder to understand, deflation and stagflation are bad signs in an economy. They generally represent an economic contraction, leading to a decrease in prosperity of a country and its people. How does this impact Americans in 2024? Following periods of heightened inflation, like we experienced at a forty-year high in 2022, goods and services aren't likely to return to their prior prices. People can expect to earn the same or less while things will become more expensive, but a little slower than they have been.

UNCLE SAM BACK FOR ANOTHER HELPING: TAXES

The last chapter discussed how taxes were not considered in Markowitz, Miller, and Sharpe's Nobel Prize-winning Capital Asset Pricing Model of investments. From Section 3, you know that taxes have a significant impact on your investments. Remember from an earlier table:

Year	Highest Federal Capital Gains Tax Rate
2023	20.0% to 23.8%

Let's look back at 2022. Perhaps your investment portfolio grew by 6% in 2022. On all accounts, you might think that your advisor had a great year since the markets were down. Let's look a little closer and see what really happened. If all your 6% gain is subject to long-term capital gain, taxes are estimated at 1.43%—bringing your net return down to 4.57%. If you live in one of the forty-two states with state capital gains tax, that could take up to another 1% or so. If you factor in 8% inflation, you "really" lost 3.2% of purchasing power from your investments.

YOUR BETTER PATH

When it comes to investing, there is no sure-fire method for avoiding taxes or inflation; however, there are investments that are better hedges against inflation. These will be discussed in the alternative investing chapter a little later in the section. The more you know about your options, the easier it will be for you to understand what you are really getting from your investments.

Of course, there is no substitute for having a strong team of advisors that includes an investment specialist who understands tax management and other advisors who are tax savvy to help you meet all your needs. One way to avoid unnecessary taxes on investments is to limit the use of mutual funds in favor of exchange-traded funds. This is explained in the next chapter.

CHAPTER 30
DON'T PAY MORE FOR LESS

AN INVESTMENT IN KNOWLEDGE PAYS THE BEST INTEREST.

—BENJAMIN FRANKLIN

The financial consulting firm Chris sold in 2017 was Jade Risk. In eastern cultures, jade symbolizes prosperity and protection. When taking risks, it seems to make sense that you would be doing it for greater prosperity and wouldn't mind a little extra protection on your journey. All Jade employees had this image on the back of their business cards.

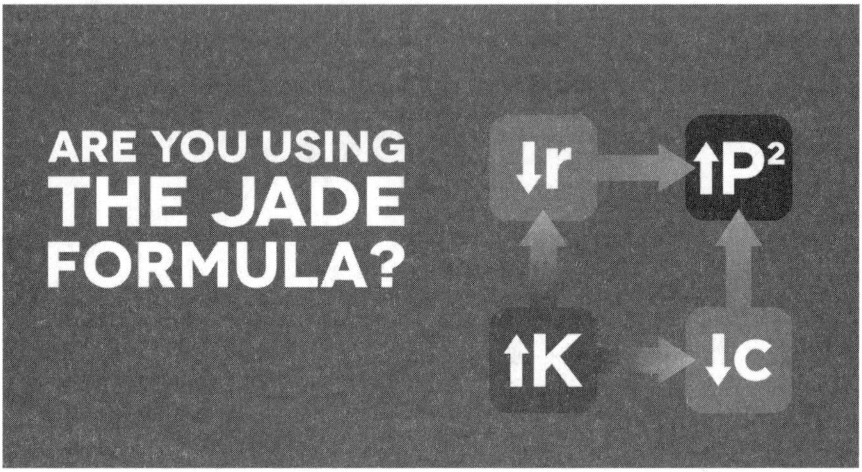

K = Knowledge. r = risk. c = costs. P = Profit + Peace of mind

The more you know about something, the less risk you take, the less things cost, and the greater your peace of mind and profitability. Beyond Wealth and Giraffe University may be different firms from Jade Risk, but the formula might as well be a law, as it holds universal applicability.

THREE-HEADED MONSTER

Mutual funds, exchange-traded funds (ETFs), and individually managed accounts (IMAs) represent three popular options for creating diversified investment portfolios. Each offers investors the ability to "outsource" the task of assembling and managing a collection of securities. Let's look at how they differ.

MUTUAL FUNDS

Mutual funds are managed by companies that invest in stocks, bonds, and other securities on behalf of individual investors. Mutual funds are essentially cooperatives of investors who pool their money for a common purpose. Investors contribute to the pool by buying shares in the fund. Each share represents an equal percentage of ownership in the fund's assets.

The fund draws from the pool not only to make investments but also to pay for the services of a fund manager (who decides if, and when, to buy and sell securities for the fund), marketing and distribution costs, custodian fees, and transaction costs. No matter how many shares of the fund the investor holds, he or she cannot control the buying and selling of securities inside the fund. Investors only control how many shares of the fund they own.

EXCHANGE-TRADED FUNDS (ETFS)

An ETF is, arguably, an evolutionary step in the life cycle of the mutual fund. Like mutual funds, ETFs are pooled investment vehicles with a specific purpose—to track an index, sector, commodity, or defined investment strategy. Unlike mutual funds, they can be bought and sold on stock exchanges the same way regular stock can be. They frequently have lower internal costs than mutual funds and can be bought and sold with no transaction fees on many platforms.

ETFs first debuted in 1993 with the SPDR S&P 500 ETF (SPY), also called the SPYDER. After paying mutual fund managers to create funds that were painstakingly assembled and managed to closely mimic the S&P 500 index, investors now had a low-cost alternative that tracked the movements of the S&P 500 index all in one neat little wrapper. ETFs initially made their name tracking popular indexes but over the years a host of different strategies have been introduced. Fast-forward to 2022 and there are now 198 ETF sponsors and over 2,800 individual ETFs in the United States alone.

INDIVIDUALLY MANAGED ACCOUNTS

IMAs are accounts that are individually managed by a professional investment manager who decides when to buy and sell securities based on the investor's stated investment strategy or goal.

Unlike mutual fund investors, managed account investors do not pool their money. Rather, they own the securities in their accounts directly. Managers may have many similar holdings with several of their clients, but each portfolio is treated separately. The investor can direct the manager to buy only certain types of investments or to avoid others. This obviously gives the investor greater flexibility and control than with a mutual fund.

ARE MANAGED ACCOUNTS WORTH THE MONEY?

Understandably, many clients are obsessed with fees associated with any type of planning. We would like to talk about the difference between price and value. In a commodity world, where all products are the same, price is important. In more complicated scenarios, price may be less important. We have charged as little as $2,500 and as much as $250,000 to clients in the last sixty days. There is truth to the saying "You get what you pay for." You should not be quick to dismiss the advantages of one investment strategy over another based purely on price. Let's build on the "knowledge" first, then we can address "risk" and "cost."

A prudent investor may ask:

- What services are included, and excluded, for this service fee?
- How does the advisor address tax management of gains/losses annually?

- What platforms can the advisor support (is there an IDF for PPLI assets)?
- Is there a minimum return or an alternative "profit share" fee arrangement?
- What family wealth, or business consulting, services do you also offer?

The answers to these questions may support higher fees in some situations.

HOW SENSITIVE IS YOUR TAX SITUATION?

With mutual funds, investors pay taxes on their pro rata share of capital gains experienced by the fund, regardless of whether they benefited from the sale of the security. Further, mutual fund managers are concerned with long-term growth. There are too many investors in the fund to concern themselves with the taxation of any individual investor.

With IMAs, the investor pays taxes only on the capital gains that they realize. Because the investor owns the securities directly, they can work with their tax advisor in ways that mutual funds do not offer. If you have loss carryforwards, unrealized gains, unique challenges (like homebuilders have) or concentrated positions, working directly with a very savvy advisor is likely a better plan.

FEES, FI, FO, FUM

As recently as the early 2010s, fees charged on IMAs and Mutual Funds were much higher than they are today, making investing much more costly. When ETFs started gaining popularity with their lower fees and ease of access, the rest of the industry had a rude awakening and had to lower fees.

Despite the downward pressure, fees for IMAs can vary greatly, as can minimum account sizes. Most firms will go below their published minimums, but it's not uncommon to see minimums of $100,000 to $1,000,000. A common fee estimate in the industry for accounts below $1 million is about 1% of assets (0.25% paid quarterly). A smaller account may have higher fees and a larger account likely pays lower fees. All fees will be disclosed either in the Firm's SEC Form ADV (for registered investment advisory firms), a prospectus (for a registered security), or a private placement memorandum (for private placements). You should never invest in anything before receiving an ADV and/or a prospectus.

Subsequent transaction costs are paid either by paying commissions on individual trades or by paying an asset-based fee on a monthly/quarterly basis. In addition to covering transactions, these fees encompass reporting, custody, and the services of a financial advisor as well. For firms that offer fee-only services, there should not be any additional charges.

Mutual funds have lower minimum investment requirements, often $1,000 or less. With a no-load mutual fund, the entire investment is placed in the fund at the time of initial purchase. With a front-end load fund, on the other hand, the investor's money is placed in the fund only after deducting a sales charge. In the case of a 3.5% load fund, the fund would invest $965 of an investor's initial $1,000.

Management fees, transaction costs, custody fees, and distribution and marketing costs (known as 12b-1 fees) are deducted automatically from the fund's assets periodically. In the bad old days, mutual fund expenses for stock-based portfolios typically ranged from 1.5% to 2% per year for no-load funds and from 2% to 3% per year for load funds.

This trend has largely reversed since the fee wars. With pressure coming from the ETF complex and investors having more access to educational information, the percentage of mutual funds purchased in 2022 that had no load fee or 12b-1 fees was 91%! In the year 2000, this number was only 46%—my, how the times have changed. The average expense ratio for actively managed stock mutual funds has dropped to 0.66% per year and the average for all equity mutual funds has fallen to 0.44%.

Which brings us to the undisputed king of low fees, the ETF. As we mentioned previously, ETFs were originally designed to give investors access to a diversified pool of investments at a low cost. In 1996, index-based equity ETFs had an average expense ratio of 0.27%, but there were transaction costs associated with buying and selling. In 2022, the average expense ratio for index-based equity and bond ETFs was a miniscule 0.05%, and transaction fees on these investments have all but disappeared on major investing platforms.

For this reason, we see many advisors and individual account managers utilizing a broader suite of ETFs to provide diversification and exposure to their clients' accounts in a cost-effective manner. Unfortunately, there isn't yet an ETF for everything, so direct investment and mutual funds still have their place.

YOUR BETTER PATH

If you remember Baskin-Robbins from your childhood, you remember why they were so popular. They had thirty-one flavors of ice cream. We are not suggesting that you need thirty-one investment accounts, but we are emphasizing that there are different types of accounts for different types of investors. Over time, investors may utilize various strategies—in different accounts.

For example, you may rely on mutual funds inside your company-sponsored retirement plan because you have no other choice. You may select those same investments inside Roth IRAs that have small account balances.

If you are a home builder, you may be willing to pay hundreds of thousands of dollars per year to have an individual manager buy lumber futures as a hedge against the costs that impact your operating business profit margins. If you have over five million dollars of non-retirement plan assets to invest, you should undoubtedly consider a private placement life insurance policy to create asset protection and tax benefits—and be able to invest within individually managed accounts or alternatives like hedge funds (covered in the next chapter).

As we explained in the beginning, the more you know, the better prepared you are to navigate these high seas. It may seem rough at times, but it will be worth it.

CHAPTER 31

ALTERNATIVE INVESTMENT STRATEGIES

In the previous chapter, you learned that individually managed accounts (IMAs) offer investors greater flexibility. This flexibility offers tax management benefits and customization to better fit the investor's situation. Traditionally, most individually managed accounts hold investments that are readily available to anyone (publicly traded securities). However, the investment world doesn't end with stocks and bonds. There are additional classes of investments that cannot be made available to the public because of their complexity or level of risk.

ACCREDITED INVESTORS

Alternative investment strategies can be offered to investors who have the financial means to survive the significant losses that can accompany riskier transactions.

Historically, these investments are only available to a class of investors known as accredited investors. To qualify as an accredited investor, an investor must be a financial institution, an affiliate of the issuer, or an individual with a net worth of at least $1 million or an annual income of at least $200,000, and the investment must not account for more than 20% of the investor's worth.

WHY INVEST IN ALTERNATIVE INVESTMENTS?

In the beginning of this section, we discussed that greater risk is generally accompanied by a potential for greater return in financial markets. Alternative investments are riskier than traditional investments, so they offer a significant risk premium (added expected return) to investors to convince them to invest. Other incentives include:

- Increased diversification by expanding portfolio to include other asset classes.
- Decreased volatility by investing in strategies uncorrelated to the stock market.
- Preservation of capital through hedging risks.

THE RISKS OF ALTERNATIVE INVESTMENTS

We mentioned that alternative investments have a higher risk than traditional investments. These may include:

- **Lack of regulation:** Most are not required to be registered with the Securities and Exchange Commission (SEC) (though many hedge fund managers choose to do so to gain access to the institutional investors that require it). It wasn't until the second half of 2022 that the Digital Commodities Consumer Protection Act authorized the CFTC to regulate digital commodities—a little too late for investors in FTX and BlockFi. This is the old-fashioned caveat emptor, or buyer (investor) beware situation.

- **Lack of transparency:** Assets held by hedge funds may not have a price quoted each day. This also means there is less liquidity, so you shouldn't have your safety net investments inside alternatives.
- **Excessive leverage:** Some managers borrow money on borrowed money. By accepting your $1,000,000 and borrowing another $1,000,000 for a project, the investors can potentially enjoy much higher returns when the project rate of return is much higher than the loan amount. Of course, the loan increases the risk of the investment because the lender gets all their money back before you get any.
- **Fraud:** There are unqualified money managers who are very good at building trust and confidence, and appealing to investors' greed. Sam Bankman-Fried is in jail for such fraud.

- **Manager selection risk:** Not all managers are equal. In fact, there is evidence that the difference in manager performance is greater than the benefit of using alternative investments.

ALTERNATIVE INVESTMENT STRATEGIES

Behind the press reports of outrageous returns and epic bankruptcies, there are sound investment strategies grouped together in the category of hedge funds. This simple term includes more than two dozen investment strategies. These investments offer access to creative structures for investments in securities or access to completely different classes of investments altogether. We are tempted to call these "Giraffe investments" because they are different, but we will refer to them as "alternatives" or "alts" to the common investment path.

ALTERNATIVE STRATEGIES THAT INVOLVE TRADITIONAL STOCKS

While many alternative strategies involve exotic investments, several strategies that rely on traditional investments underneath the surface include:

- **Options trading:** Instead of buying an individual stock, you can buy "positions" that bet on future movement. Calls allow you to buy the stock at a certain price in the future. Puts allow you to sell at a certain price. These allow investors to make more money with stock volatility than they would from owning the stock. Of course, they come with more risk, as 90% of options expire worthless. To mitigate risk, there are straddles, strangles, iron condors, butterfly spreads, calendar spreads, and ratio spreads. These are very complicated, but do offer unique benefits and opportunities to savvy, risk-tolerant investors.

- **Short selling:** This is essentially betting against a stock. You agree to borrow and sell stock you don't even own at a certain price. If the price goes down, you win. If it goes up, you must buy the stock to return to the owner, which can be very costly. The cautionary poem about short selling in a business school text is "he who sells what isn't his'n, must buy it back or go to pris'n."
- **Margin/leveraged Investing:** This is a credit/debit card variation of the two above. You use your existing portfolio as collateral, take a loan from your investment firm, and purchase more shares. Could be great, could be a disaster.
- **Strategy-specific funds:** These include global macro, long/short equity, event-driven, distressed debt, arbitrage, fixed-income, quantitative, commodities, sector-specifics, and probably a dozen more that were invented as we wrote this book.

INVESTING IN STARTUPS AND EARLY-STAGE COMPANIES

Our clients who have created generational wealth didn't get there from investing; they got there from creating. This could mean starting a business, developing innovative technology, creating inspiring art, or even writing a book about wealth! Our clients have an appreciation for entrepreneurs and innovators, but their interest in start-ups isn't purely altruistic (read ***Be the Giraffe***, Chapter 13—Taste the Pee). Successful and influential people often invest in startups because they can bring more than just capital. They leverage their knowledge and contacts in an industry, as well as their experience, to the new company.

This is how Chris has been able to raise millions from healthcare experts and physicians to invest in Mission 3A and from successful entrepreneurs to invest in Fundify, where they can bring immediate and additional value to the businesses.

Our wealthiest clients understand the "Casino model." When gamblers go into a casino, sometimes they win and sometimes they lose. When lots of gamblers go into a casino, the casino always wins.

Many savvy investors know that "the house always wins," so they are skeptical of the stock market and the banks that control them. This is why nearly every family office and successful entrepreneur is interested in "deal flow"—so they can see what new *Shark Tank*-type companies are out there for them.

WAYS TO "GET IN EARLY"

There are many ways to invest in startups. Each has its unique application. This list of categories, with examples of individuals and firms we have invested in, worked with, sat on panels with, or discussed collaboration, should help you understand the landscape.

1. **Angel Investing:** This involves individual investors providing funding to startups in exchange for equity ownership. Famous examples are your "Sharks," Mark Cuban, Daymond John, Lori Grenier, Barbara Corcoran, Robert Herjavec, and Kevin O'Leary. Josh Chodniewicz (of Fundify.com) and Carey Ransom (of BankTech Ventures) are two successful angel investors we know personally. They have leveraged their own experience as "angels" into profitable businesses where you could invest alongside them.
2. **Venture Capital:** Venture capital firms pool funds from multiple investors to provide financing to high-potential startups in exchange for equity. Mohanjit Jolly and Anand Prasanna started Iron Pillar (www.ironpillarfund.com) to give investors an opportunity to invest in technology startups in India. With offices in India, Dubai, and Palo Alto, they help investors identify growth companies before they become household names.
3. **Crowdfunding:** Platforms like Kickstarter and Indiegogo allow individual investors to contribute small amounts of money to startups in exchange for rewards or equity. This is a great way to access startups with very little capital. The big challenge is determining which companies to select.

4. **Accelerators and Incubators:** These programs provide support, mentorship, and sometimes funding to startups in exchange for equity. Chris has lectured and mentored multiple companies through the UCLA Anderson School Accelerator. These opportunities are great places for investors to volunteer their time to get to know founders early in their journey—and to meet the other mentors from the alumni group.
5. **Private Placements:** This involves investing directly in a private placement offering by a startup company, typically through a broker-dealer or investment bank.
6. **Corporate Venture Capital:** Some established corporations have venture capital arms that invest in startups to gain access to new technology or strategic partnerships.
7. **Syndicate Investing:** Investors can participate in a syndicate led by an experienced angel investor or venture capitalist to collectively invest in a startup. In a syndicate, investors are pitched individual deals for direct participation (instead of being part of a fund where they receive a piece of every deal). Before Cerberus acquired SGI (a syndicate), Chris had many interactions with SGI's founder who was investing across the globe in emerging markets.

8. **Peer-to-Peer Lending:** Some platforms allow individuals to lend money to startups in exchange for interest payments, similar to traditional lending but with higher risk.
9. **Venture Studio:** This is a blend of venture capital, angel investing, and accelerator. Studios will build, finance, and accelerate the growth of startups within their own platform. They identify needs, evaluate different opportunities, and develop concepts around them. Chris has invested directly in Mission 3A Venture Studio (mission3a.com). With his healthcare background, Chris was intrigued with the idea of improving healthcare outcomes by leveraging technology and low-cost app development. The 3A founders had successfully sold businesses to Apple and GoPro before turning their technology expertise toward helping improve healthcare outcomes in rural and underserved areas.
10. **Equity Crowdfunding:** This involves investing in startups through online platforms that allow individuals to buy shares or convertible debt in early-stage companies.

THE SHIFTING TIDE OF STARTUPS

Until recently, only wealthy "accredited investors" could invest in private offerings. Because finding startups, reviewing their business plans, and negotiating terms for investment was so time intensive, venture capital, private equity and startup funds were the only realistic options. As the only games on the street, they had large minimum investments, charged outrageous fees, and created structures where investors pay for all overhead while the fund retains 20% to 30% of the upside without any risk.

With the advent of Reg CF (Crowdfunding), these large minimum investment and high net worth "accredited" status barriers have been largely removed. The legislation permits crowdfunded assets from non-accredited investors to be pooled and invested in an individual startup. Despite being passed several years ago, Reg CF has not been extensively utilized by private equity firms and venture capitalists who still focus on high-net-worth and ultra-high-net-worth clientele.

Now, there are almost 100 crowdfunding platforms where everyday investors can dip their toes into the water of startup investing. Unfortunately, the challenge of sorting through the business plans and selecting companies is still quite problematic. Wealthy investors can rely on private equity firms and venture capitalists to guide them, but regulations precluded the crowdfunding platforms from making decisions on behalf of their investors. Ironically, the class of investors who need the most assistance were once precluded from getting that help from people who could help them. What did we say earlier about the house always winning? We digress.

At the end of 2023, everyday investors had a big win that few people may have realized. The SEC gave its first approval for a subscription-based, discretionary investment, crowdfunding platform for startups. With as little as $1 per month (though we think most people will invest $50 to $5,000 per month), you can set up an account at Fundify.com. Every month, Fundify will pool the dollars and buy shares of startups on behalf of its subscribers. Every investor gets the same price. After a year, you will have a portfolio of dozens of startups. After five years, you will own hundreds of startups. This is such an exciting opportunity that both authors have invested in Fundify and subscribed to invest through the platform as well!

CHAPTER 32

SIMPLE IS HARD

THERE IS NO GREATNESS WHERE THERE IS NO SIMPLICITY, GOODNESS, AND TRUTH.

—LEO TOLSTOY

The concept of investment efficiency is not one you will find in most finance textbooks. In Section 1, you learned that financial planning, and by association investing, doesn't need to be that difficult. . .until your life gets more complicated. As part of this acceptance, you must also recognize that general information in books, newspapers, articles, online, or on television is likely to be inappropriate for you because it is geared toward the average American's financial needs. If you can adopt a disruptive philosophy, you can easily expand your planning opportunities to include investments that can give your family greater flexibility, leverage, and efficiency.

INVESTING IS A MARATHON, NOT A SPRINT

If investing doesn't need to be that complicated, why are so many people intimidated by the idea of investing? There are endless "sources" pushing the next great strategy that will change our lives. For most people simply having a plan will put you ahead of your peers. The investing universe consists of endless options, but the ability to identify the ones that are most relevant to your needs will provide far more value than the endless parade of hot tips that can cloud your view. As your wealth grows, so will the complexity of your needs and your investment choices.

Consider the lessons we learned from CAPM and MPT of the types of risk, the risk reward paradigm, and diversification as metrics to determine what is right for you. In a prior section we discussed the differences between mutual funds, exchange-traded funds and IMAs. But those are just a few tools you can choose to execute on your plan. As you embark on your investment journey, there are a few things we advise you to consider.

KEEP IT SIMPLE, UNTIL IT HURTS

For many investors, we recommend two key principles: invest early and invest often. Albert Einstein noted that "compounding of interest is one of humanity's greatest inventions." By setting a cadence of investment, whether it's $100 per paycheck or $10,000, everyone can benefit from one of the greatest wonders of the world, compounding interest. Once you have had a chance to work through your budgeting exercises and determine how much you can invest on a monthly, quarterly, or annual basis, we implore you to set up an automatic investment plan. One of the greatest contributors to accumulation of wealth over the years is discipline. This can be achieved by creating a routine around investing in your goals.

There are many ways to achieve discipline, but the two most common ways are creating an automatic investment plan in a brokerage account (after-tax) and taking advantage of your company's qualified retirement plan. By utilizing a brokerage account, you gain the benefit of accessibility to the capital you have invested at the drawback of having to pay capital gains taxes on realized gains. With company-sponsored retirement programs, we enjoy the benefits of tax-advantaged investment accounts and the bonus of employer matches. We don't know about you, but we are hard pressed to find places to achieve an immediate 100% return on capital outside of employer-sponsored retirement programs. If your employer offers a match to your 401(k) or 403(b) contributions, please take advantage of this benefit. It's literally free money.

BENCHMARK BLUES

Most investment professionals measure themselves against a benchmark—the median of returns by all investors in a marketplace. If you are below the benchmark, you are in the bottom half of performers. If you beat the benchmark, you are in the top half of performers. For some reason, it has become "acceptable" for investment advisors to "meet" or slightly exceed the benchmark. When you consider that it's easy to create a simple asset allocation and invest using low-cost exchange-traded funds, it doesn't make sense to pay a professional advisor to get you "average" returns. This low-cost ETF approach can minimize fee drag on your portfolio.

As your wealth grows, the benefits to deploying your capital in new and more sophisticated ways start to have more compelling outcomes. At this point, it may be wise to employ the services of a savvy investment professional who is well versed in navigating financial markets and tax optimization strategies. Individually managed accounts can provide access to unique investment options and the ability to manage your tax liabilities. They may also provide access to many of the alternative investments we highlighted in the previous section.

THE NEED FOR EFFICIENT INVESTMENTS

Investment efficiency is the theory that one investment can help address two concerns. This is important because you have limited time, you don't have a crystal ball, and you'd like to do something with your life other than worry about and obsess about your money.

TWO BIRDS, ONE STONE

What does this mean? We love investments that are designed to build wealth while reducing taxes. We appreciate investments that inherently offer us some level of asset protection without the need for costly legal work. We like tax-favored investments that can be used for multiple things, like college saving or retirement income. We absolutely love investing within structures that allow us to access the funds if we need them, but also pass to our heirs without gift or estate taxes, and without any fees or delays.

NO FREELOADING PARTNERS

Your hidden partner in nearly everything you do is Uncle Sam. He doesn't directly contribute to your companies or investments, but he certainly gets his fair share (if not a whole lot more—that's up to you to decide after completing Section 3). Investments can be more "efficient" when they have less tax friction. Savvy investors consider all the potential threats to their assets, not the least of which is tax. Roth accounts are extraordinary (thus the reason you want to explore back-door strategies to Roths). When used correctly, real estate can be fantastic. An often-misunderstood tax haven for many of the ultra-high-net-worth families is cash value life insurance (CVLI). For investors with at least $5 million to invest, private placement life insurance is a home run. For assets not in any of those vehicles, advisors creatively utilize trusts, LLCs, and corporations to accomplish "income sharing" as a crafty leverage or arbitrage technique.

ALWAYS LIFT WITH (SOMEONE ELSE'S) LEGS

Our parents always taught us to have a strong work ethic. Our investments, planning, and businesses need to be lazy! We don't mean that they don't work. We mean they don't have to do all the work themselves. You shouldn't spend $25,000 to accomplish a goal if it could be handled for $5,000—or for $0. We are not suggesting using the low-cost provider every chance we get. That would be silly since we work with a value-based fee model. We are only the low-cost provider when we are competing with a Big Five accounting firm or international consulting firm. We digress.

We are talking about using our exemptions for asset protection instead of spending large sums of money on legal planning (that may not even be as strong as the federal or state protections). Roth IRAs, retirement plans, annuities, and life insurance offer asset protection for free.

GOOD FENCES MAKE FOR GOOD NEIGHBORS

Hope for the best, but plan for the worst—but not in a doom and gloom kind of way. Efficient investments can also be your safety net. After doing more than one thousand financial plans, we have learned that there is only one certainty. Nothing ever goes according to plan. Life will throw us a series of curveballs. We must design plans with an expectation that they will need to change. By using flexible investments that can serve multiple roles, we use tools that are more likely to adapt to the clients' future needs with less pain, aggravation, and cost.

YOUR BETTER PATH

Section 1 discussed the importance of leverage in accumulating wealth. It's no surprise that people get obsessed with investing. There are thousands of magazines, blogs, and subscriptions available to eager investors. The idea of putting your hard-earned money into some vehicle, partnership, fund, or investment and letting someone else work his butt off and turn your money into even more money is beautiful. It is the exact definition of leverage.

However, there are millions, if not billions, of people trying to master the investment world. People are looking for trends and inefficiencies all the time. Firms dedicate billions of dollars to finding small bits of arbitrage across the world. In the end, our experience is that the more people obsess over investments, the more of their lives they lose.

Our hope for you with your investing is to get some leverage, create some efficiency, and maintain a decent amount of flexibility along the way. If you can save taxes, create some protections, avoid disasters, and provide for heirs with a couple well-placed investments, and spend 10% – 20% of your money on investments with more upside (like Fundify.com or inside a venture studio), you can get your life back and probably end up with similar or better results than those who spend their lives with CNBC on 24/7.

INVESTING SUMMARY

When it comes to starting your investing journey, simple is better than interesting. Create your plan and get started. But interesting is always more fun, and with a solid foundation, your investments will start to get more interesting as you accumulate wealth.

1. **Simplicity Is the Key:** Investing isn't about having the fanciest strategy developed by Nobel laureates. It's about growing your wealth through discipline and consistency. It begins by understanding your risk tolerance, time horizon, and investment objectives.
2. **Know the Terrain:** Don't put all your faith in old Wall Street theories or talking heads on CNBC. After all, they have their own agenda and products to push. Understanding the real costs of investing means balancing your return for a given level of expense.

3. **Reduce Tax Pain:** Using retirement plans, tax-efficient investments, trusts, and corporate structures provides flexibility when tax planning and can help transition your estate to your heirs with minimal pain.
4. **Your Investment Toolbox:** Start with the basics using ETFs to replicate benchmarks. As you get more sophisticated, you might want to add some power tools to the mix with IMAs or alternatives. Remember, what works for your friend might not suit your style, yet.
5. **Dive into Alternatives When You Are Ready:** Once you've got the basics down, consider exploring the Investment equivalent of off-the-beaten-path travel. Alternative investments can be riskier, like trying street food in a foreign country, but they can also offer unique rewards.
6. **Don't Forget about the Little Guy:** Most of the wealth in the world was created by people who started or invested in small businesses. Platforms like Fundify can be a great diversification and wealth-building tool.
7. **Get Good Advice:** If you are just starting to invest, you may need only a handful of ETFs in your portfolio to get the job done. As your wealth grows, the tax situation becomes more complicated, and risk appetite changes, so finding a knowledgeable wealth manager to add to your team can pay dividends.

Investing is a marathon, not a sprint, and the right strategies can make it a rewarding one. Keep at it, stay informed, and remember, even Warren Buffett had to start somewhere.

As you consider your investment strategy, we ask that you leverage these simple steps:

INVESTING CHECKLIST

	Define your financial goals and time horizon.
	Consult with a financial advisor to integrate your investment plan into your total plan.
	Set an investment budget and regularly contribute (build good habits).
	Create multiple vehicles for investing (Roth, 401[k], cash value insurance, after tax account).
	Create a diversified investment portfolio that matches your risk tolerance.
	Consider alternative investments (like Fundify.com) for added diversification and increased potential.
	Consider tax implications and seek tax-efficient investment strategies.
	Monitor and review your investments periodically.

SECTION 7

PLAN FOR SUCCESS

"SOMEDAY" IS A DISEASE THAT WILL TAKE YOUR DREAMS TO THE GRAVE WITH YOU.

—TIMOTHY FERRISS

Arnold Schwarzenegger is the most famous bodybuilder of all time, with seven Mr. Olympia titles (1970–75, 1980). Have you ever heard of Ronnie Coleman? He is the second-most-famous body builder, despite having won eight consecutive Mr. Olympias (1998-2005) and winning twenty-five years more recently. What's the difference? Marketing, of course.

Ronnie never said anything as timeless as "I'll be back," but he did have some epic sound bites. Picture a 5'11" man, weighing 300 pounds, with less than 1% body fat. Now, imagine the high-pitched pubescent voice of your teenager coming out of his mouth screaming, "Everybody wants to be a bodybuilder, but nobody wants to lift no heavy-ass weights! But I do!" This smart-ass comment is supported by a very intelligent statistic:

> Everyone wants to be wealthy, but 99% of the population will not be in the top 1%.

In Ronnie's case, he talks about moving heavy-ass weights. Training to become the best in the world is time-consuming, physically painful, and requires you to pretty much sacrifice everything else in your life.

We have shared countless statistics about worry, stress, depression, frustration, distrust, and pain—around money, financial planning, and all the threats to your wealth. The purpose of ***giraffeMONEY Essentials*** is to show you that financial planning can be done quickly and painlessly so you can get back to what matters most.

Are you willing to take a few small steps toward moving into the top 1%, or maybe the top 0.01%, with your planning? If you are, the following chapters and offers will help you maximize the return you get for your investment of time and money.

CHAPTER 33

DIFFERENT ISN'T ALWAYS BETTER, BUT BETTER IS ALWAYS DIFFERENT

THE MEASURE OF INTELLIGENCE IS THE ABILITY TO CHANGE.

—ALBERT EINSTEIN

If this is starting to sound redundant, good! Throughout this book, ***Be the Giraffe,*** and ***giraffeMONEY***, we explained that there are countless ways to build wealth. We showed you many ways to protect your money from outside threats. Unfortunately, the biggest threat to your money isn't external. **The biggest obstacle to financial success is inaction**.

It's not your fault that you haven't done your planning. . .yet. It's unfortunate that so many people get so little, if any, of their planning done. Perhaps it's because the entire process looks so daunting. *Not even Hannibal would dare take giraffes over those mountains.*

This shouldn't be the case—and it doesn't have to be for you now. The investment, insurance, legal, and accounting industries have done everyone a disservice. By making the planning seem so complicated, advisors make themselves appear more valuable. The truth is at least 90% of the planning for any family worth less than $30,000,000 can be done in three to six months.

DON'T LET PERFECT BE THE ENEMY OF GOOD.

We know we are talking about your hard-earned wealth. It makes sense that you don't want to make mistakes. After helping thousands of families and businesses, we can say with absolute certainty that no plan has ever gone to term. Life happens, things change. You can't predict life perfectly, so you can't plan perfectly.

In ***Essentials,*** we focused on strategies and tools that offer you a great deal of flexibility. Nothing we suggested can't effectively be "undone" or "repurposed" as life throws you all kinds of not-so-subtle curveballs. Take the pressure off yourself and find comfort in your imperfect planning.

If you can get 90% of your planning done with 10% of the effort, then we should start there. Using the tools and checklists we've provided at the end of each section will help you collect your data and your thoughts before you start thinking about what your 90% looks like and start checking off the boxes.

SMALL STEPS TOWARD BIG RESULTS

Congratulations on reading this far. You should be commended for your diligence and applauded for surviving our silly, if not obscure, jokes. Money is an important part of our lives, but it shouldn't dominate our thoughts and actions. Here are some short steps for you to keep in mind as you move forward:

Step 1: Decide what you want to accomplish

Step 2: Find someone to help you

Step 3: Set a date for completion

Step 4: Continue learning in a way that works for you

Step 5: Review the plan at least annually

CHAPTER 34

SEEK A BETTER PATH

SUCCESS IS OFTEN A MISSTEP IN THE RIGHT DIRECTION.

—AL BERNSTEIN

To set the direction for your planning, you should reflect on the lessons in ***giraffeMONEY Essentials***:

1. **Craft *YOUR* Long-Term Vision**: One of the first steps in creating a plan is developing a long-term financial vision and setting clear goals for personal and business financial success.
2. **Take Inventory of Your Current Situation:** To plan your journey to reach your financial goals, you need to start from where you are. Making a list of assets, liabilities, and planning documents will be important. Feel free to use our Full Perspective Form at www.beyondwealth.pro/resources.

3. **Protect Your Current and Future Wealth:** Lawsuits and other threats can derail our progress. Review the state and federal exemptions, as well as legal tools, that can help protect your assets as you build wealth.
4. **Avoid Unnecessary Taxes:** Understand the tax implications of all financial decisions and explore strategies to minimize income and capital gains taxes. Get a tax professional to review your last two years' tax returns and offer suggestions.
5. **Protect Your Family:** The "Golden Age of Estate Planning" is scheduled to sunset in 2026 when the laws change. More than 90% of Americans have living trusts and powers of attorney. For families worth $30 million, simple SLATs can eliminate all unnecessary taxes.
6. **Insure Your Family's Stability and Success:** Review existing life and disability insurance. If you don't have insurance and would like us to help you get quotes for convertible term, cash value insurance, disability, or even Private Placement Life Insurance, you can email us at tony@beyondwealth.pro.
7. **Review Your Investments:** Have a qualified financial or investment professional look at your retirement plan, personal holdings, and corporate investment accounts. Develop good habits by saving monthly.

Pay attention to asset protection, tax efficiency, and creative ways to maximize upside while managing downside risk. Explore any opportunity for Roths and "Roth-like" investments. Consider interesting opportunities, like Fundify.com, for 5% – 10% of your savings.

8. **Flexibility:** Don't forget to layer into your planning strategies and tools that can have multiple uses. These will include Roths, LLCs, SLATs, and life insurance.
9. **Take Action & Share Your Goal Today:** People who take one step toward a goal within fifteen minutes of setting it are considerably more likely to reach it. Those who write down their goals and share them with someone are 44% more likely to reach their goals than people who don't. Increase your odds by texting a friend or family member now!
10. **Be Curious—Continue Learning:** Elephants may never forget but giraffes never stop evolving. Acknowledging that financial markets and regulations change and making a commitment to lifelong learning will keep you ahead of the herd. By joining a community of like-minded giraffes, you will get continued support and encouragement. If you own a business, www.GiraffeU.com might be worth considering.

CHAPTER 35

READY, SET. . .

GREAT IS THE ART OF BEGINNING, BUT GREATER IS THE ART OF ENDING.

– HENRY WADSWORTH LONGFELLOW

You should feel fantastic about getting through this book. We are impressed that we got this far ourselves. Now, the greatness of your new beginning on a better path is before you. Changing your philosophy and planning to incorporate ***giraffeMONEY Essentials*** may seem overwhelming. There are many different steps to be taken within each of the paths to building wealth. The key to doing it FASTER is doing something. This book includes only a partial list of the potential strategies that you could use because it is more important that you get the high-impact things done, not everything. There is no way one person could handle the challenge of planning alone. There is no way to do all this planning without help. This is why the most important thing you can do is assemble the right team to work with you.

Remember that every giraffe began as a member of the herd until one person saw things differently—which allowed them to money differently, business differently, and life differently. If you dedicate yourself to the process, you can be the person to break your family free from the herd.

IF YOU STILL AREN'T CONVINCED. . .

We set out to write ***giraffeMONEY Essentials*** to alleviate your fears and to encourage you to do things you may have been afraid to do before reading it. If this still seems overwhelming and you would like us to help you, we would be honored to help you find someone in your area or connect you with a specialist to handle any unique challenges you have. If you would like to work with us directly at Beyond Wealth, we are flattered. Feel free to email tony@beyondwealth.pro or register for a free consultation at www.BeyondWealth.pro.

It has been our honor and privilege to guide you on this journey. We are excited to see where it takes you. Keep us posted on your progress as you. . .

Elevate Your Perspective

See a Better Path; and

Be the Giraffe!

ABOUT THE AUTHORS

CHRIS JARVIS

Chris Jarvis is a mathematician and financial engineer with thirty years of experience helping millionaire entrepreneurs and billionaire families build and preserve wealth.

During his actuarial career, Chris created and managed tax-efficient risk solutions for hundreds of companies—including one of the world's large auto manufacturers—before selling his firm in 2016.

Authoring eighteen books (including the bestseller ***Be the Giraffe***), delivering a viral TEDx Talk ("Surviving Ain't Thriving") with over 4 million views, and writing for *Entrepreneur* and *Forbes* gave Chris fantastic exposure and access. Jarvis has worked with thousands of affluent clients and their attorneys, accountants, agents, and advisors. Along the way, he discovered the unique paths to the highest levels of success—and the common pitfalls that hold most people back from reaching their financial goals.

"I wrote ***giraffeMONEY*** and ***giraffeMONEY Essentials*** to demonstrate how common financial, legal, and tax strategies are grossly inadequate for the high-net-worth clients. Hiring the most well-known firms does not guarantee you are getting the best advice. I know because those same firms have brought me in to help solve their clients' most complicated problems."

Chris has lectured at the Anderson School (UCLA) Accelerator, University of Rhode Island College of Business, and Venture Café at MIT. He sits on the dean's advisory council for the University of South Carolina School of Medicine and the advisory board of the prestigious IC^2 Institute at the University of Texas-Austin, exploring economic development solutions for rural communities.

Chris holds an honors degree with distinction in Applied Mathematics from the University of Rhode Island and a Master of Business Administration with a concentration in Finance and Entrepreneurship from UCLA. Chris holds the CERTIFIED FINANCIAL PLANNER™ certification.

Jarvis has created many avenues for affluent clients to find better solutions. He is a co-founder of Beyond Wealth (financial engineering and planning), a venture partner at Mission 3A (venture studio), and an early investor in Fundify (startup investing and funding). Through Giraffe University, Chris coaches a select group of entrepreneurs through the complexities and interconnectedness of their money, businesses, and personal lives as they pursue ambitious and impactful projects.

LEARN MORE

https://ChrisJarvis.me/about-chris/

TONY ASSADI

Tony Assadi, CFA, CFP® has nearly twenty years of investment, financial planning, insurance, and banking experience. This diverse background gives his clients a unique perspective on building, preserving, and transferring wealth.

His financial journey began with a fascination for the markets and a desire to understand how wealth is created. Uncharacteristically, Tony started with technology as the Director of Product and Strategy for DST Brokerage Solutions. Leading a team of 200 people, he developed software solutions for many large retail financial firms. As the Head of the Wealth Management Practice at NTT Data Consulting, he interacted with the strategic planning departments of many wealth management firms. After spending years "on the inside" of financial services, Tony realized a big problem —and an even bigger opportunity.

"When I say I grew up in financial services I mean that quite literally. My father is a long-time insurance executive at the highest level. I started attending industry conferences long before I could vote – or drive. My career has spanned nearly two decades supporting hundreds of financial firms with technology and consulting solutions. Though financial, insurance, and investment firms would all have you think they are different, they all have one thing in common: they are product driven aiming to maximize leverage. People often build things they can call their own then find ways to sell as much of it as possible to as many people as possible. Though leverage is a key to success (when you are applying it to your assets), it can have a different effect when leverage is applied to you.

In a world that is becoming increasingly reliant on technology, the opportunity for customization is sacrificed on the altar of efficiency. In writing ***giraffeMONEY Essentials***, I hope to show people how to identify the solutions they need and to help them only pay for what they actually need — nothing more, nothing less."

Tony Assadi holds a Bachelor's Degree in Applied Physiology from Towson University and a Masters in Business Administration with a concentration in Finance from the R.H. Smith School of Business at the University of Maryland. He is a Chartered Financial Analyst (CFA) Charterholder as well as a CERTIFIED FINANCIAL PLANNER™ practitioner.

Tony grew up in Baltimore, MD where he now lives with his wife Lauren. He splits time between Baltimore and Dallas/Tyler, TX where he works with his partner Chris Jarvis and the innovative team at UBank.

FIND TONY

www.BeyondWealth.pro/about

"You're not too big. This room is too small!"